Selected Poems

Roy Fuller was born in Failsworth, Lancashire in 1912 and grew up in Blackpool. On leaving school, he trained as a solicitor. He married in 1936, and his son John was born the following year. He served in the Royal Navy during the Second World War and then spent his working life with the Woolwich Building Society, of which he became a director. His prolific literary output included eighteen collections of poetry, nine novels and four volumes of memoirs, as well as books for children. He was Professor of Poetry at Oxford from 1968 to 1973, and served on the BBC Board of Governors for seven years from 1972 and as Chairman of the Arts Council Literature Panel, 1976–7. He was awarded the CBE and the Queen's Gold Medal for Poetry in 1970. Roy Fuller died in 1991.

John Fuller was born in 1937. A poet, novelist and critic, from 1966 to 2002 he was Fellow and Tutor in English at Magdalen college, Oxford, where he is now Emeritus Fellow. His *Collected Poems* were published in 1996, and his *Stones and Fires* won the Forward Prize in 1997. The latest of his nineteen collections of poetry, *Pebble and I* (Chatto) and *Writing the Picture*, with the photographer David Hurn (Seren), appeared in 2010. His critical book *Who is Ozymandias? And Other Puzzles in Poetry* was published by Chatto in 2011.

Neil Powell was born in 1948. He has published seven books of poetry with Carcanet Press, including a *Selected Poems* (1998) and his latest collection, *Proof of Identity* (2012). His authorised critical biography *Roy Fuller: Writer and Society* was published in 1995. His other biographical works include *George Crabbe: An English Life* (Pimlico, 2004), *Amis & Son: Two Literary Generations* (Macmillan, 2008) and a centenary life of Benjamin Britten (to be published by Hutchinson in 2013).

W0009751

Also available from Carcanet Press

Roy Fuller, *Crime Omnibus*
Neil Powell, *Roy Fuller: Writer and Society*

Roy Fuller

Selected Poems

Edited by John Fuller

With a preface by John Fuller and
an afterword by Neil Powell

CARCANET

First published in Great Britain in 2012 by
Carcanet Press Limited
Alliance House
Cross Street
Manchester M2 7AQ

www.carcanet.co.uk

ISBN 978 1 84777 121 6

The publisher acknowledges financial assistance from Arts Council England

Supported by
ARTS COUNCIL
ENGLAND

Typeset by XL Publishing Services, Tiverton
Printed and bound in England by SRP Ltd, Exeter

CONTENTS

From *A Lost Season* (1944)

2
1945–1962

from *Epitaphs and Occasions* (1949)

from *Counterparts* (1954)

3
1963–1977

4
1977–1989

from *New and Collected Poems* (1985)

from *Subsequent to Summer* (1985)

from *Consolations* (1987)

from *Available for Dreams* (1989)

from *Last Poems* (1993)

A NOTE ON THE TEXT

Original volume publication of these poems is clearly shown in the Contents list, though not repeated elsewhere. The texts of the poems, despite their ascription to the individual collections in which they appeared, are in the first three sections drawn from the sometimes revised versions of *New and Collected Poems* (1985).

John Fuller

PREFACE

I suppose that I first became aware of my father's early fame in 1943, when at the age of six I came across his uniformed photograph in the local evening paper and his name in the *Radio Times*. The war for me had meant a happy exile to my grandparents' house in Blackpool, interspersed with uncomfortable experiences of transient digs during his naval training in Lee-on-Solent, Warrington, Harrogate and Aberdeen, keeping myself occupied as best I could and listening to his records on a wind-up gramophone kept under the bed: Ella Fitzgerald's 'Black Coffee' or the neglected Countess in *The Marriage of Figaro*. For him, the war brought separation, drudgery, fear and uncertainty, but also the compensation of success for his poems. His second collection, *The Middle of a War*, published when he was thirty, made his name: a new impression of 1,500 copies was needed within two months of publication.

During his subsequent posting to Nairobi as an air fitter in the Fleet Air Arm I missed him probably less than he missed my mother and me (his absence was simply part of what he had become, like the unfamiliarly deep upper lip when they shaved off his moustache) but for him that exile gave him further crucial experiences of alienation and political uncertainty:

When we have pissed away the marble walls,
And turned a foreign vandyke in the suns,
And lions wander in the ruined halls
And come and lick the barrels of our guns,
And the last letter has arrived and been
Forgotten, and the nights are dreamless –

                               Then
Shall we be free? And turn for home, as lean
And baffled wolves turn for their starving den?
Or shall we merely look upon our nails
And see what kind of beast we have become;

And weep at that: or, if our nature fails,
Shrug, and descend to dancing and the drum?

This possibility of a civilisation succumbing to barbarism is from 'The Legions' in *A Lost Season* (1944) and chimes with similar sentiments in poems from Auden's Cavafy period, which my father, though an immense admirer of Auden, could not yet have read.

The imperial débâcle postulated by 'The Legions' was a natural outcome of his experience of Kenya and of the general feeling of the conscripted military forces that once Hitler had been defeated then the Tories should be turned out, too. For my father (long a convinced and active socialist) the class divisiveness of British society was perfectly symbolised by the arrangements for the officers and other ranks on the troopship carrying him to Africa. He witnessed the discontent and great desire for change at first hand: 'It is the beginning of something. What is lacking is the confidence that things *can* be changed, that the people at the top both in this life & in civvie street can be deposed. The reason for this lack of confidence is the lack of knowledge of the *machinery* of revolution. Every bourgeois intellectual who has 'gone over' to the proletariat & who is not in the *ranks* has betrayed the proletariat: he has precious knowledge, precious, which can transform the anger & disgust & disillusion' (unpublished journal, 1942). He felt similarly about the evidence of imperialist attitudes in Kenya.

After the war, my father took up his old job in the legal department of the Woolwich Building Society, in one sense a return to the upper decks. He embarked on a renewed programme of writing and the continuation of the process of self-education which had kept him sane on that troopship, when he was reading Thackeray and Balzac and Jacobean drama in his hammock. During this post-war period, with our family together again and resettled in Blackheath in suburban London, I became more and more aware of his punishing daily schedule (familiar to anyone who has attempted such a dual life), getting up at 6.30 to write poems, then reading for book reviews and longer articles in the evening. He even used to come home from Woolwich in the middle of the day, so that he could have a lunch that suited his precarious digestion, take a brief rest and do some more literary work. Regular habits of this kind, with the maintenance of commonplace books and other notebooks, lasted for the rest of his life. He was once more, and more than ever, an organisation man, with an endless willingness to serve his profession. In 1948, for example, he had in preparation both *Questions and Answers in Building Society Law and Practice* (Franey & Co.) and *With My Little Eye: A Mystery Story for Teen Agers* (John Lehmann).

His journalism and broadcasting at first show little slackening of the political attitudes of his youth. In a long and generally very positive article on the still-unpopular George Eliot, written in 1945, for example, he attacked her last novel for a perceived evasiveness which he cannot help associating with his own now ambiguous position: 'It is difficult to avoid seeing Zionism in *Deronda* as a naïve substitute for socialism, as evidenced by its lean and fanatic partisans, the tawdry, serious meetings, Deronda's first prejudice against it, his love for the Jewish (read 'proletarian') girl, his discovery that he has been a 'proletarian' all the time. He is, in fact, the perfect left-wing intellectual; sheepishly making assignations with the revolutionaries and hating anyone, particularly of the working-class, touching him, toying with the movement like a surfeited cat with a cod's-head.' The last comic image is a classic commonplace Fullerian touch, an irony designed to defuse the more serious self-accusation that might be levelled at him as such a left-wing intellectual.

The Roman metaphor of 'The Legions' quoted above is continued in poems like 'Translation' written in 1949 (see p. 57) but the intervening four years of post-war disillusion have now led to a crucial and decisive distancing from political commitment:

> The ruling class will think I am on their side
> And make friendly overtures, but I shall retire
> To the side farther from Picra and write some poems
>   About the doom of the whole boiling.

This is the classic position of disaffected Roman poets, but it has a particular significance for a politicised British writer of the 1930s who has given up hope of revolution. Though coming to maturity during the war, my father had been writing for well over a decade. Born in 1912, and having been articled to a firm of solicitors since the age of sixteen when he left school, he had already completed a volume of poems as early as September 1934, which he submitted to the Hogarth Press ('Their merit and originality are considerable,' said Leonard Woolf). His eventual first collection had appeared in 1939. Even by then, the poems of his first political period had been largely replaced by poems from his surrealist period. The traumas of war effectively encouraged an approach quite different from either of these somewhat programmed modes. This was to tell the truth as he saw it, either in the light of the most credible and adaptable ideas of historians, philosophers and scientists, or simply as it occurred to him in the circumstances of common daily life. It is in this area, where ideas and feelings luminously encounter each other, that most of his best work continues to be found.

As I grew up, I of course got to know my father's work pretty well, almost as it appeared. I read that novel *'for Teen Agers'* at the age of twelve; fed him on holiday with similes which he then inserted into a poem, with a charming acknowledgement; collaborated with him on French translations and an abortive play; and in the middle of my teens started to write poems myself. I have never known whether this early closeness has made me a privileged or partial judge of his work. We always read and commented on each other's poems, and in due course, when my own interests were established, our criticisms were blessedly free from flattery or offence. His advice was of infinite technical benefit to me, coming as it did from such a tender, generous and humorous man. I could not have had a better father.

Choosing the poems for this selection has been difficult. I have had to judge afresh the faults of the familiar, to temper undue fondness for favourites, and distinguish between essentially indistinguishable successes. The corpus is large (a *Complete Poems* might easily reach over 950 pages) so that some very broad pruning has had to be done. In general, I have wanted to maintain variety, while giving sufficient elbow room to his sonnet sequences, where completeness is an advantage. I have included little from before the war, and little, too, of the often occasional immediately postwar poems, where it seems to me that pressure of other work narrowed their effect. There was a breakthrough in the 1950s with new themes from myth and history, and a surprising metaphysical deepening in *New Poems* of 1968. Many of the later volumes really need to be read through in bulk (the annotatory tercets of *From the Joke Shop*, for example, or the sonnets of *Available for Dreams*), and the whole idea of sequence begins to take a grip on his mode of writing. Once the pen begins to 'run on', everything is grist to the meditative mill: the expanding universe, the dwindling family past, dreams, Music Hall celebrities, the wildlife of a suburban garden, ill health, literary quirks, domestic routines, the ever-changing quality of the sky at dusk. He is not the only poet to have so dignified ordinary experience, but the insistent honesty of the way in which he does it became a whole way of writing.

Honesty (or is it the inexhaustible frankness of apologia?) was also a principle behind the volumes of memoirs (collected as *The Strange and the Good*, 1989) but it never descended to the intimate or the confessional. It was more interested, as were his novels, in the social aspects of human relations. Even the somewhat Kafkaesque predicaments of the adulterous solicitor in *Image of a Society* or the guilty father in *The Father's Comedy* are about conflicts with institutions as much as with individuals. The memoirs are concerned with the humorous eccentricities of others, and the supposed moral failings of the author.

One extreme exemplum of this watchful outlook is my father's despair at follies that appeared to devalue the culture he worked so hard to acquire and preserve. To sing in a choir, like his maternal grandmother (indeed, to sacrifice her unusual talent to a life of wifely support and public service), was of inestimable virtue; to pursue a specious fame in ignorance of the best in the tradition, or with exhibitionist self-confidence, was unspeakable. At times, in television commentaries contemporary with his role as a Governor of the BBC, for example, or when he served on the Arts Council and notoriously resigned on issues of funding choices, he did speak up, very often in a voice of rebuke and irritation. These institutions would, in an ideal world, be responsible for the very best in the arts and in popular culture that could be found and promoted. My father was affronted when they were not. It was a sign of 'descending to the drum'.

This was not the conservative position that it might seem to be ('I have never voted Tory in my life,' my father once said to me, after a conversation in which I must have seemed to rebuke him for some perceived failure of tolerance) but the testament of an achieved belonging. He was an idealist, who had vividly experienced all the inimical forces, inherited and circumstantial, that drive someone towards the eventual establishment of a considered way of life, a good that he firmly believed should be available to all. To a great extent he was shy and felt no personal need to wage battles; but he was ready to stand up for what he believed in. The organisation man within him cultivated a mask of gregarious wit in order to survive potentially hostile environments. I grew to recognise this mode in conferences and committees, and it seemed utterly at odds with the poet who sat down of an evening by the large sitting-room window of his bungalow, with his notebook and a Scotch-and-soda on the arm of his chair and Scriabin on the turntable.

In making my selection, in which I have favoured the more fictive and philosophical elements in his work, or emphasised the themes of immanence, I have greatly benefited from the advice of Neil Powell, who has continually reminded me of the need to be representative and to remember old anthology pieces that may not be familiar to new readers. Although I favour the fresh power and eloquence of his considered meditative poems, with their quirky detail and openness to strange lines of thought, there is also a great cumulative power in the more circumstantial pieces, with their journal-driven honesty and wonderful eye for oddities. The ironical, the wry, the rueful, the self-deprecatory: honesty often led him down this road, with its occasionally diminished returns. I would often accuse him of deliberately over-exposing a cartoon valetudinarian persona, over-conscious of his age and with a low level of cultural tolerance. To go with this persona (which I failed to recognise in the man himself) he developed an idiosyncratic vocabulary, combining the Latinate with Lancashire dialect, which his adopted syllabic metres accommodated in unabashed parentheses and inversions.

But just when the reader might think that this late stylistic manner has become too ingrained for comfort, a great surge of lyrical feeling will blow through everything, like a wind through leaves, and the reader comes to see that the caution and discrimination of prosiness is simply there as a foundation for the revelatory discoveries of the intelligence. This is particularly true of sonnets, to which my father throughout his writing life devoted so much of his attention. I wanted to include whole long sequences ('Mythological Sonnets', 'The Historian' and 'Later Sonnets from the Portuguese') because it is here that the accumulating and reflective manner works most effectively. The last of these is his final substantial poem, unsettling in its point of view (imagining the poet as the estranged wife of a poet), but rich in the implications that reach from this donnée, through the spider-haunted domesticity of the setting and the searching scientific questioning, into an assessment of the precariousness of life and love.

John Fuller

1

1938–1944

To M.S., Killed in Spain

Great cities where disaster fell
In one small night on every house and man,
Knew how to tell the fable from the flesh:
One crying O, his mouth a marble fountain;
Her thigh bones in immortal larva
At compass points, the west and east of love.

Necks bent to look for the seditious geese,
Or over blocks, gazing into freedom;
Heads all alike, short noses, brows
Folded above, the skin a leather brown;
Wrists thick, the finger pads worn down
Building oppression's towering stone.

Now uncovered is the hero,
A tablet marks him where his life leaked out
Through grimy wounds and vapoured into air.
A rusty socket shows where in the night
He crammed his torch and kept by flame at bay
Dark, prowling wolves of thought that frightened him.

The poor outlasted rope and crucifix,
We break the bones that blenched through mastic gold;
And excavate our story, give a twist
To former endings in deliberate metre,
Whose subtle beat our fathers could not count,
Having their agile thumbs too far from fingers.

> I fear the plucking hand
> That from our equal season
> Sent you to war with wrong
> But left me suavely wound
> In the cocoon of reason
> That preluded your wings.

As the more supple fin
Found use in crawling, so
Some new and rapid nerve
Brought close your flesh to brain,
Transformed utopia
To death for human love.

And my existence must
Finish through your trauma
The speechless brute divorce
Of heart from sculptured bust:
Turn after five acts' drama
A placid crumpled face.

I see my friend rising from the tomb,
His simple head swathed in a turban of white cloth.
The vault is spotted with a brownish moss,
One corner broken, fallen to the floor,
Whereon I read SPAIN as he advances like
An invalid, changed terribly with pain.

A quiet room holds him, half-raised from the bed,
Eyes big and bright, a waxwork, and the blood
Of waxworks running down his cheek. Two candles
Rock their light. The bed is moving, tilting,
And slips him rigidly to take a new position,
The elbow sharp, the skin a yellow leaf.

The third time he stands against a summer country,
The chestnuts almost black in thunderous air,
The silver green of willow lining dykes
Choked with flesh. He moves along the furrows
With labourer's fingers, spreading death against
The imperishable elements of earth.

What is the meaning of these images?
The wish to leave all natural objects richer,
To quicken the chemistry of earth, to be
Immortal in our children. Such desires
Are bodies in a pit, the rotting and bloody
Backwash of a tidal pestilence.

The scalpel in my back
That broke my uneasy dream
Has extended in a scythe,
Is passing through the quick,
Forcing like strychnine
My body to its curve.

The future is not waking,
Nor the name and number
Of distorted figures, and knowledge
Of pain. It is the breaking
Before we slumber
Of the shaping image.

So from the nightmare, from
The death, the war of ghosts,
Those chosen to go unharmed
May join the tall city, the swan
Of changing thoughts
Set sailing by the doomed.

August 1938

Mapping this bay and charting
The water's ribby base
By individual smarting
And walks in shifting sand,
We note the official place;
Dover with pursed-up lips
Behind the purple land
Blowing her little ships
To danger, large and bland:

Aeroplanes softly landing
Beyond the willowed marsh:
The phallic lighthouse standing
Aloof with rolling eye

From shingle flat and harsh:
And sequinned on the coast
Beneath the usual sky
The pleasure towns where most
Have come to live or die.

Far off the quinsied Brenner,
The open hungry jaw
Of Breslau and Vienna
Through day-old papers join
The mood of tooth and claw
To useless coastal road,
The excursion to Boulogne
And valedictory ode,
The hairy untanned groin.

Oh never is forever
Over this curving ground
When both the dull and clever
Leave for their town of graves,
And on the dissolving mound
By snowy seabirds signed
'Through all routes quit these waves,'
Lonely among his kind
The local spirit raves.

After the Spanish Civil War

The common news tells me
How I shall live:
There are no other values.
In central Spain I lie,
Fed by what earth can give
Through an iron mesh.

The roads are blown to air;
Tracks drawn to wire with the chill
Of this snowy winter.
Along the air and wire
The news comes, even evil,
Fainter and fainter.

Though events stop happening,
There remain the forces:
The wrestlers immense outside,
Oiled and immobile; wrong
Red between love and faces
In broken shade.

To My Brother

A pistol is cocked and levelled in the room.
The running window opens to the sounds
Of hooters from the Thames at Greenwich, doom

Descends the chimney in the rustling grounds
Of soot. The Globe edition of Pope you gave me
Is open on the chair arm. There are bounds

To feeling in this suburb, but nothing can save me
Tonight from the scenic railway journey over
Europe to locate my future grave: the

Arming world rushes by me where you hover
Behind right shoulders on the German border,
Or at the Terminus removing a cover,

Taking perhaps your memories, like a warder,
The memories of our responsible youth,
To give the refugees a sense of order.

My real world also has a base of truth:
Soldiers with labial sores, a yellowish stone
Built round the common into cubes, uncouth

Reverberations from a breaking bone,
The fear of living in the body. Is it
Here we start or end? Tonight my own

Thoughts pay a merely temporary visit
To the state where objects have lost their power of motion,
Their laws which terrify and can elicit

A furious tale from casual emotion,
Where life with instruments surveys the maps
Of cut-out continent and plasticine ocean,

Far from the imminent and loud collapse
Of culture, prophesied by liberals,
Whose guilty ghosts can never say perhaps.

This kind of world Pope, with his quartz and shells,
Constructed in his azure Twickenham grotto,
Which in the daytime entertained the belles,

But glowed and writhed to form a personal motto
At night, with brute distraction in its lair;
The mirrors flattering as part of the plot: 'O

Alex, you are handsome; you have power
First to arrange a world and then to abstract
Its final communication; virtues shower

From the exercise of your genius; the pact
Of friendship is good and all your enemies only
In opposition to civilization act.'

When I am falsely elevated and lonely,
And the effort of making contact even with you
Is helped by distance, the life is finely

Shown which holds on contract, and the true
Perish in cities which revolve behind
Like dust.

The window explodes, and now
The centre land mass breathes a tragic wind.

Autumn 1939

Cigar-coloured bracken, the gloom between the trees,
The straight wet by-pass through the shaven clover,
Smell of the war as if already these
    Were salient or cover.

The movements of people are directed by
The officious finger of the gun and their
Desires are sent like squadrons in the sky,
    Uniform and bare.

I see a boy through the reversing lens
Wearing a shirt the colour of his gums;
His face lolls on the iron garden fence
    Slobbering his thumbs.

I have no doubt that night is real which creeps
Over the concrete, that murder is fantasy,
That what should now inform the idiot sleeps
    Frozen and unfree.

The Barber

Reading the shorthand on a barber's sheet
In a warm and chromium basement in Cannon Street
I discovered again the message of the hour:
There is no place for pity without power.

The barber with a flat and scented hand
Moved the dummy's head in its collar band.
'What will you do with the discarded hair?'

The mirror showed a John the Baptist's face,
Detached and side-ways. 'Can you tell me how,'
It said, 'I may recover grace?

'Make me a merchant, make me a manager.'
His scissors mournfully declined the task.
'Will you do nothing that I ask?'

'It is no use,' he said, 'I cannot speak
To you as one in a similar position.
For me you are the stern employer,
Of wealth the accumulator.
I must ignore your singular disposition.'

He brushed my shoulders and under his practised touch
I knew his words were only a deceit.
'You spoke to me according to the rules
Laid down for dealing with madmen and with fools.'

'I do my best,' he said, 'my best is sufficient.
If I have offended it is because
I never formulate the ideal action
Which depends on observation.'

'And do you never observe and never feel
Regret at the destruction of wealth by war?
Do you never sharpen your razor on your heel
And draw it across selected throats?'

He smiled and turned away to the row of coats.
'This is your mackintosh,' he said, 'you had no hat.
Turn left for the station and remember the barber.
There is just time enough for that.'

First Winter of War

There is a hard thin gun on Clapham Common,
Deserted yachts in the mud at Greenwich,
In a hospital at Ealing notices
Which read WOMEN GASSED and WOMEN NOT GASSED.

The last trains go earlier, stations are like aquaria,
The mauve-lit carriages are full of lust.
I see my friends seldom, they move in nearby
Areas where no one speaks the truth.

It is dark at four and on the peopled streets,
The ornamental banks and turreted offices,
The moon pours a deathly and powdered grey:
The city noises come out of a desert.

from
The Middle of
a War
1942

It is dark at twelve: I walk down the up escalator
And see that hooded figure before me
Ascending motionless upon a certain step.
As I try to pass, it will stab me with a year.

To My Wife

The loud mechanical voices of the sirens
Lure me from sleep and on the heath, like stars,
Moths fall into a mounting shaft of light.
Aircraft whirr over and then the night stays quiet;
The moon is peeled of cloud, its gold is changed
On stone for silver and the cap of sky
Glitters like quartz, impersonal and remote.
This surface is the same: the clock's bland face,
Its smiling moustaches, hide the spring, knotted
Like muscles, and the crouching jungle hammer.

The same but so different with you not here.
This evening when I turned from the clothes you left,
Empty and silk, the souls of swallows flickered
Against the glass of our house: I felt no better
Along the tree-massed alleys where I saw
The long pale legs on benches in the dark.
It was no vague nostalgia which I breathed
Between the purple colloids of the air:
My lust was as precise and fierce as that of
The wedge-headed jaguar or the travelling Flaubert.

But I only encountered the ghosts of the suburb,
Those ghosts you know and who are real and walk
And talk in the small public gardens, by the tawdry
Local monuments; the Witch and Big Head
And the others, fleeting and familiar as
Our memories and ambitions, and just as dead.
Being alone they stopped me; Big Head first.
Removing her unbelievable hat, she showed me
What before I had only conjectured, and she whispered:
O lucky you – you might have been born like this.

I knew it was true, but, hurrying on, the Witch
Lifted her cane and barred the way: she is
Lean and very dirty but hanging round
That skeleton are rags of flesh still handsome.
Moving her lips madly and in a foreign tone she said:
Oh do not hope, boy – you will come to this.
I ran, being certain that she had not erred,
Back to our room where now the only noise
Is the icy modulated voice of Mozart
And the false clock ticking on the mantelpiece.

Now in the bubble of London whose glass will soon
Smear into death, at the still-calm hour of four,
I see the shadows of our life, the Fates
We narrowly missed, our possible destiny.
I try to say that love is more solid than
Our bodies, but I only want you here.

I know they created love and that the rest
Is ghosts; war murders love — I really say.
But dare I write it to you who have said it
Always and have no consolation from the ghosts?

Autumn 1940

No longer can guns be cancelled by love,
Or by rich paintings in the galleries;
The music in the icy air cannot live,
The autumn has blown away the rose.

Can we be sorry that those explosions
Which occurring in Spain and China reached us as
The outer ring of yearning emotions,
Are here as rubble and fear, as metal and glass,

Are here in the streets, in the sewers full of people?
We see as inevitable and with relief
The smoke from shells like plump ghosts on the purple,
The bombers, black insect eggs, on the sky's broad leaf.

For these are outside the deathly self
Walking where leaves are spun across the lips
Bitten against tears which bridge no gulf,
Where swans on the flat full river are moving like oared ships.

Death is solitary and creeps along the Thames
At seven, with mists and changing moons;
Death is in the music and the paintings, the dreams
Still amorous among the dispersing guns.

But where the many are there is no death,
Only a temporary expedient of sorrow
And destruction; today the caught-up breath —
The exhalation is promised for tomorrow.

And changed tomorrow is promised precisely by
The measure of the engendered hate, the hurt
Descended; the instinct and capacity
Of man for happiness, and that drowned art.

Soliloquy in an Air Raid

The will dissolves, the heart becomes excited,
Skull suffers formication; moving words
Fortuitously issue from my hand.
The winter heavens, seen all day alone,
Assume the colour of aircraft over the phthisic
Guns.

But who shall I speak to with this poem?

Something was set between the words and the world
I watched today; perhaps the necrotomy
Of love or the spectre of pretence; a vagueness;
But murdering their commerce like a tariff.

Inside the poets the words are changed to desire,
And formulations of feeling are lost in action
Which hourly transmutes the basis of common speech.
Our dying is effected in the streets,
London an epicentrum; to the stench
And penny prostitution in the shelters
Dare not extend the hospital and bogus
Hands of propaganda.

Ordered this year:
A billion tons of broken glass and rubble,
Blockade of chaos, the other requisites
For the reduction of Europe to a rabble.
Who can observe this save as a frightened child
Or careful diarist? And who can speak
And still retain the tones of civilization?

The verse that was the speech of observation –
Jonson's cartoon of the infant bourgeoisie,
Shakespeare's immense assertion that man alone
Is almost the equal of his environment,
The Chinese wall of class round Pope, the Romantic
Denunciation of origin and mould –
Is sunk in the throat between the opposing voices:

I am the old life, which promises even less
In the future, and guarantees your loss.
And I the new, in which your function and
Your form will be dependent on my end.

Kerensky said of Lenin: *I must kindly*
Orientate him to what is going on.
Watching the images of fabulous girls
On cinema screens, the liberal emotion
Of the slightly inhuman poet wells up in me,
As irrelevant as Kerensky. It is goodbye
To the social life which permitted melancholy
And madness in the isolation of its writers,
To a struggle as inconclusive as the Hundred
Years' War. The air, as welcome as morphia,
This 'rich ambiguous aesthetic air'
Which now I breathe, is an effective diet
Only for actors: in the lonely box
The author mumbles to himself, the play
Unfolds spontaneous as the human wish,
As autumn dancing, vermilion on rocks.

Epitaph on a Bombing Victim

Reader, could his limbs be found
Here would lie a common man:
History inflicts no wound
But explodes what it began,
And with its enormous lust
For division splits the dust.
Do not ask his nation; that
Was History's confederate.

ABC of a Naval Trainee

A is the anger we hide with some danger,
Keeping it down like the thirteenth beer.
B is the boredom we feel in this bedlam.
C is the cautious and supervised cheer.

D is the tea dope and E English duping,
Too feeble for folly, too strong for revolt.
F is the adjective near every object,
The chief of desires for both genius and dolt.

G is the gun which can kill at, say, Greenwich
If fired at St Martin's, and H is our hate
Non-existent behind it wherever we wind it.
I is the image of common man's fate.

J is the Joan or the Jill or Joanna,
Appearing in dreams as a just-missed train.
K is the kindness like Christmas tree candles,
Unexpected and grateful as poppies in grain.

L is the lung or the limb which in languor
Rests after work and will soon be exposed
To M which is murder, a world rather madder,
Where what we pretend now's as real as your nose.

from The Middle of War 1942

N is the nightingale's song that we're noting
When the sky is a lucid darkening silk,
When the guns are at rest and the heart is a cancer
And our mouths make O at the moon of milk.

Then we remember, no longer a number,
We think of our duties as poets and men:
Beyond us lie Paris, Quebec, Rome, where diaries
Of millions record the same troubles and pain.

S is the silence for brooding on violence.
T is the toughness imparted to all.
U is the unit that never will clown it
Again as the lonely, the shy or the tall.

V is the vastness: as actor and witness
We double our role and stammer at first.
W is war to start off the quarries –
Our everyday hunger and every night thirst.

X is the kiss or the unknown, the fissure
In misery stretching far back to the ape.
Y is the yearning for Eden returning;
Our ending, our Z and our only escape.

Defending the Harbour

We form a company to help defend
The harbour. Close against the quay a landed
Monster of a trawler huddles, grey, with sides
Flaking, and aft a grey untidy gun.
Mist shines the cobbles, dulls our waiting boots.

A climbing street links sea and town: we watch
Its pathetic burden of human purpose. All
The faces in my section are thumbed and known
As a pack of cards, and all the characters
Group and speak like a bad familiar play.

And nothing happens but the passage of time,
The monotonous wave on which we are borne and hope
Will never break. But we suspect already
The constant ache as something malignant and
Descry unspeakable deeps in the boring sand.

And on the quay, in our imagination,
The grass of starvation sprouts between the stones,
And ruins are implicit in every structure.
Gently we probe the kind and comic faces
For the strength of heroes and for martyrs' bones.

Royal Naval Air Station

The piano, hollow and sentimental, plays,
And outside, falling in a moonlit haze,
The rain is endless as the empty days.

Here in the mess, on beds, on benches, fall
The blue serge limbs in shapes fantastical:
The photographs of girls are on the wall.

And the songs of the minute walk into our ears;
Behind the easy words are difficult tears:
The pain which stabs is dragged out over years.

A ghost has made uneasy every bed.
You are not you without me and *The dead
Only are pleased to be alone* it said.

And hearing it silently the living cry
To be again themselves, or sleeping try
To dream it is impossible to die.

The End of a Leave

Out of the damp black light,
The noise of locomotives,
A thousand whispering –
Sharp-nailed, sinewed, slight,
I meet that alien thing
Your hand, with all its motives.

Far from the roof of night
And iron these encounter;
In the gigantic hail
As the severing light
Menaces – human, small,
These hands exchange their counters.

Suddenly our relation
Is terrifyingly simple
Against our wretched times,
Like a hand which mimes
Love in this anguished station
Against a whole world's pull.

The Middle of a War

My photograph already looks historic.
The promising youthful face, the matelot's collar,
Say 'This one is remembered for a lyric.
His place and period – nothing could be duller.'

Its position is already indicated –
The son or brother in the album; pained
The expression and the garments dated,
His fate so obviously preordained.

The original turns away: as horrible thoughts,
Loud fluttering aircraft slope above his head
At dusk. The ridiculous empires break like biscuits.
Ah, life has been abandoned by the boats –
Only the trodden island and the dead
Remain, and the once inestimable caskets.

Another War

Pity, repulsion, love and anger,
The vivid allegorical
Reality of gun and hangar,
Sense of the planet's imminent fall:

Our fathers felt these things before
In another half-forgotten war.

And our emotions are caught part
From them; their weaponed world it is
They should have left to the abyss
Or made an image of their heart.

Spring 1942

Once as we were sitting by
The falling sun, the thickening air,
The chaplain came against the sky
And quietly took a vacant chair.

And under the tobacco smoke:
'Freedom,' he said, and 'Good' and 'Duty'.
We stared as though a savage spoke.
The scene took on a singular beauty.

And we made no reply to that
Obscure, remote communication,
But only looked out where the flat
Meadow dissolved in vegetation.

And thought: O sick, insatiable
And constant lust; O death, our future;
O revolution in the whole
Of human use of man and nature!

Harbour Ferry

The oldest and simplest thoughts
Rise with the antique moon:
How she enamels men
And artillery under her sphere,
Eyelids and hair and throats
Rigid in love and war;
How this has happened before.

And how the lonely man
Raises his head and shudders
With a brilliant sense of the madness,
The age and shape of his planet,
Wherever his human hand,
Whatever his set of tenets,
The long and crucial minute.

Tonight the moon has risen
Over a quiet harbour,
Through twisted iron and labour,
Lighting the half-drowned ships.
Oh surely the fatal chasm
Is closer, the furious steps
Swifter? The silver drips

From the angle of the wake:
The moon is flooding the faces.
The moment is over: the forces
Controlling lion nature
Look out of the eyes and speak:
Can you believe in a future
Left only to rock and creature?

Goodbye for a Long Time

A furnished room beyond the stinging of
The sea, reached by a gravel road in which
Puddles of rain stare up with clouded eyes:

The photographs of other lives than ours;
The scattered evidence of your so brief
Possession; daffodils fading in a vase.

Our kisses here as they have always been,
Half sensual, half sacred, bringing like
A scent our years together, crowds of ghosts.

And then among the thousand thoughts of parting
The kisses grow perfunctory; the years
Are waved away by your retreating arm.

And now I am alone. I am once more
The far-off boy without a memory,
Wandering with an empty deadened self.

Suddenly under my feet there is the small
Body of a bird, startling against the gravel.
I see its tight shut eye, a trace of moisture,

And, ruffling its gentle breast the wind, its beak
Sharpened by death: and I am yours again,
Hurt beyond hurting, never to forget.

Troopship

Now the fish fly, the multiple skies display
Still more astounding patterns, the colours are
More brilliant than fluid paint, the grey more grey.

At dawn I saw a solitary star
Making a wake across the broken sea,
Against the heavens swayed a sable spar.

The hissing of the deep is silence, the
Only noise is our memories.

        O far
From our desires, at every sweaty port,
Between the gem-hung velvet of the waves,
Our sires and grandsires in their green flesh start,
Bend skinny elbows, warn: 'We have no graves.
We passed this way, with good defended ill.
Our virtue perished, evil is prince there still.'

The Photographs

The faces in the obscene photographs
Gaze out with no expression: they are like
The dead, who always look as though surprised
In a most intimate attitude. The man
And woman in the photograph have faces
Of corpses; their positions are of love –
Which we have taken. I remember how
Once, coming from the waves, I found you chill
Beneath the *maillot* in a sun-warmed house;
And on such memories are now imposed
The phantasies engendered by these two.
Evening: the rows of anxious aircraft wait,
Speckled with tiny brown and crimson birds;

The plain extends to an escarpment lit
Softly as by a steady candle flame;
And then there is the great curve of the earth
And, after, you, whom two seas and a war
Divide.
          The dust blows up. As long as those
Photographs poison my imagination
I shall not dare to catch my countenance
In any mirror; for it seems to me
Our faces, bodies – both of us – are dead.

The Green Hills of Africa

The green, humped, wrinkled hills: with such a look
Of age (or youth) as to erect the hair.
They crouch above the ports or on the plain,
Beneath the matchless skies; are like a strange
Girl's shoulders suddenly against your hands.
What covers them so softly, vividly?
They break at the sea in a cliff, a mouth of red:
Upon the plain are unapproachable,
Furrowed and huge, dramatically lit.

And yet one cannot be surprised at what
The hills contain. The girls run up the slope,
Their oiled and shaven heads like caramels.
Behind, the village, with its corrugated
Iron, the wicked habit of the store.
The villagers cough, the sacking blows from the naked
Skin of a child, a white scum on his lips.
The youths come down in feathers from the peak.
And over all a massive frescoed sky.

The poisoner proceeds by tiny doses,
The victim weaker and weaker but uncomplaining.
Soon they will only dance for money, will
Discover more and more things can be sold.

What gods did you expect to find here, with
What healing powers? What subtle ways of life?
No, there is nothing but the forms and colours,
And the emotion brought from a world already
Dying of what starts to infect the hills.

The Giraffes

I think before they saw me the giraffes
Were watching me. Over the golden grass,
The bush and ragged open tree of thorn,
From a grotesque height, under their lightish horns,
Their eyes were fixed on mine as I approached them.
The hills behind descended steeply: iron-
Coloured outcroppings of rock half-covered by
Dull green and sepia vegetation, dry
And sunlit: and above, the piercing blue
Where clouds like islands lay or like swans flew.

Seen from those hills the scrubby plain is like
A large-scale map whose features have a look
Half menacing, half familiar, and across
Its brightness arms of shadow ceaselessly
Revolve. Like small forked twigs or insects move
Giraffes, upon the great map where they live.

When I went nearer, their long bovine tails
Flicked loosely, and deliberately they turned,
An undulation of dappled grey and brown,
And stood in profile with those curious planes
Of neck and sloping haunches. Just as when,
Quite motionless, they watched I never thought
Them moved by fear, a wish to be a tree,
So as they put more ground between us I
Saw evidence that these were animals
With no desire for intercourse, or no
Capacity.

Above the falling sun,
Like visible winds the clouds are streaked and spun,
And cold and dark now bring the image of
Those creatures walking without pain or love.

The Plains

The only blossoms of the plains are black
And rubbery, the spiked spheres of the thorn,
And stuffed with ants. It is before the rains:
The stream is parched to pools, occasional
And green, where tortoise flop; the birds are songless;
Towers of whirling dust glide past like ghosts.
But in the brilliant sun, against the sky,
The river course is vivid and the grass
Flaxen: the strong striped haunches of the zebra,
The white fawn black, like flags, of the gazelles,
Move as emotions or as kindly actions.
The world is nothing but a fairy tale
Where everything is beautiful and good.

At night the stars were faint, the plateau chill;
The great herds gathered, were invisible,
And coughed and made inarticulate noises
Of fear and yearning: sounds of their many hooves
Came thudding quietly. The headlights caught
Eyes and the pallid racing forms. I thought
Of nothing but the word *humanity*:
And I was there outside the square of warmth,
In darkness, in the crowds and padding, crying.
Suddenly the creamy shafts of light
Revealed the lion. Slowly it swung its great
Maned head, then – loose, suède, yellow – loped away.
O purposeful and unapproachable!
Then later his repugnant hangers-on:
A pair of squint hyenas limping past.
This awful ceremony of the doomed, unknown

And innocent victim has its replicas
Embedded in our memories and in
Our history. The archetypal myths
Stirred in my mind.

        The next day, over all,
The sun was flooding and the sky rose tall.
Where rock had weathered through the soil I saw
A jackal running, barking, turning his head.
Four vultures sat upon the rock and pecked,
And when I neared them flew away on wings
Like hair. They left a purple scrap of skin.
Have I discovered all the plains can show?
The animals gallop, spring, are beautiful,
And at the end of every day is night.

Askari's Song

At dusk when the sky is pale,
Across a three-years' journey
I can see the far white hill
Which in my land is like a
Conscience or maker.

At dusk when cattle cross
The red dust of the roadway,
I smell the sweetish grass,
Half animal, half flowers,
Which also is ours.

At dusk the roads along
The separating plains are
So sad with our deep song
I could expect the mountain
To drift like a fountain,

And, conquering time, our tribe
Out of the dust to meet us
Come happy, free, alive,
Bringing the snow-capped boulder
Over their shoulder.

The White Conscript and the Black Conscript

I do not understand
Your language, nor you mine.
If we communicate
It is hardly the word that matters or the sign,
But what I can divine.

Are they in London white
Or black? How do you know,
Not speaking my tongue, the names
Of our tribes? It could be as easily a blow
As a match you give me now.

Under this moon which the curdled
Clouds permit often to shine
I can see more than your round cap,
Your tallness, great eyes and your aquiline
Nose, and the skin, light, fine.

The British must be wicked:
They fight. I have been brought
From our wide pastures, from
The formal rules of conduct I was taught;
Like a beast I have been caught.

If only I could tell you
That in my country there
Are millions as poor as you
And almost as unfree: if I could share
Our burdens of despair!

For I who seem so rich,
So free, so happy, am
Like you the most despised.
And I would not have had you come
As I most loath have come.

Among our tribe, like yours,
There are some bad, some good –
That is all I am able to say:
Because you would not believe me if I could
Tell you it is for you, the oppressed, the good
Only desire to die.

Convicts Working on the Aerodrome

Curls powdered with chalk like a black Roman bust
This prisoner, convicted of a lust
For maize, is whipped to building a great shed
For bombers; and bears the earth upon his head.

The Tribes

I think of the tribes: the women prized for fatness,
Immovable, and by a sympathetic
  Magic sustaining the herds,
  On whose strange humps sit birds;

And those with long dung-stiffened capes of hair,
And those that ceremonially eat their dead;
  The ornamental gashes
  Festered and raised with ashes;

The captured and dishonoured king compelled
To straddle a vertical and sharpened stake,
  Until, his legs hauled at,
  The point burst from his throat;

And all the prohibitions and the cheapness
Of life so hardly got, where it is death
   Even to touch the palace
   And poison expresses malice.

Now in the white men's towns the tribes are gathered
Among the corrugated iron and
   The refuse bins where rats
   Dispute with them for scraps.

Truly, civilization is for them
The most elemental struggle for bread and love;
   For all the tabus have gone,
   It is man against man alone.

On waste plots and in the decrepit shanties
They begin to discover the individual,
   And, with the sense in time
   Of Adam, perpetrate crime.

The most horrible things you can imagine are
Happening in the towns and the most senseless:
   There are no kings or poison,
   Are laws but no more reason.

Sadness, Theory, Glass

My poignant coffee does not last the twilight.
Gazing across the wide street through the central
Island of palms, I see the tight silk sky
As green as caterpillars, fretted by
The silhouettes of banks and consulates.
Cast up by war upon this neutral shore
I feel I should deliver a summing-up
Of all the passion, boredom, history,
Of all the suddenly important lives;
A rounded statement like Cézanne's of apples.

I wish I were as sure as he appears,
And wonder if the awful gaps in feeling,
Defects of seeing and experience,
Will vanish retrospectively, and this
Slight poetry, like a convex mirror, hold
A cosmos, Lilliputian but exact.

I see the future like a theory –
The proof of pamphlets, as ordained erectness
After an age of stooping, or the knowledge
Of murderous glaciers in a million years.
The future is tomorrow, but today
I fold my blanket and that moment is
Immense: I walk across the airfield and
The aircraft, like stuffed birds, are there for ever,
Horrible to the touch. The present is
A lucid but distorting medium,
As though the cunning of perspective had
Been lost by nature and all was flat and wild
And terribly more truthful. Only the past
Is real, because it stays as sadness, like
Old age remembering sexually its youth.
There is no luxury of sentiment –
Simply regret, as those regret in bedlams
Their last concession to their mania.

But we shall reach at last the day of death
Or hear guns die seditiously to silence.
There is a time when on reality
The vision fits, and sadness, theory, glass,
Fuse, and the mass directs its destiny.
The integration is the action, I
Can only scribble on the margin: here
We saw strange southern stars revolve above
The struck ship swaying from the pointed convoy;
Here kitted-up for sun, here snow; and strangely
Realized here that out of all the world
Only one other in our life would know us.

Shore Leave Lorry

The gigantic mass, the hard material,
That entering our atmosphere is all
Consumed in an instant in a golden tail,
Is not more alien, nor the moon more pale:
The darkness, countries wide, where muscled beasts
Cannot link fold on fold of mountains, least
Mysterious: the stars are not so still.
Compared with what? In low gear up the hill
The lorry takes its load of strange wan faces,
Which gaze where the loping lion has his bases,
Like busts. Over half the sky a meteor falls;
The gears grind; somewhere a suffering creature calls.

The Coast

In the garden of the aerated water factory
Is an iron fountain and the doves
Come to its lip to drink.
Outside the totos are begging for five-cent pieces;
Boys whose faces are done in sepia, the places
Round their eyes and the irises still running.
One of them is in the fifth class at the Government School:
He wants to be a teacher and tells me
That London is very cold.
This white town is at the mouth of a river
Which holds a star-shaped island;
And all the islands of the coast
Have satisfying shapes
As, flat and green, they float upon the water.
The palms make brittle noises in the wind;
At night they are prodigious plumes; among them
The sailing crescent moon glows,
And clouds which in the daytime would be white
Fume across the stars.

In the garden I think of things
For which these are inadequate images.
The white doves in the sunlight flutter in the blown
Spray from the fountain.
There is no substitute for the harsh and terrible
Facts of the time, which only longing
And sadness cloak,
And which have grown meaningless and commonplace.
My thoughts wander to the strong and desirable
Body of a girl shown as she arranged her blanket,
The swollen and fibrous, frightening leg of a beggar,
And on the road to the hospital
The bloody negro borne by his friends.
Round them stretch the lovely and legendary islands,
The jewel-coloured sea, and far,
Cold Europe.

The Petty Officers' Mess

Just now I visited the monkeys: they
Are captive near the mess. And so the day
Ends simply with a sudden darkness, while
Again across the palm trees, like a file,
   The rain swings from the bay.

The radio speaks, the lights attract the flies,
Above them and the rain our voices rise,
And somewhere from this hot and trivial place
As the news tells of death, with pleasant face,
   Comes that which is not lies.

The voices argue: *Soldiers in the end*
Turn scarecrows; their ambiguous figures blend
With all who are obsessed by food and peace.
The rulers go, they cannot order these
   Who are not disciplined.

O cars with abdicating princes: streets
Of untidy crowds: O terrible defeats!
Such images which haunt us of the past
Flash on the present like the exile's vast
    Shivers and fleshy heats;

But never coincide. Do they approach?
Upon that doubt I'm frightened to encroach –
Show me, I say, *the organizations that*
Will change the rags and mob into the state,
    Like pumpkin into coach.

The voices make no answer. Music now
Throbs through the room and I remember how
The little pickaxe shapes of swallows swerve
From balconies and whitewashed walls; a curve
    Of bird-blue bay; a dhow:

Small stabbing observations! And I know
(The cheap song says it on the radio)
That nerves and skin first suffer when we part,
The deep insensitive tissues of the heart
    Later, when time is slow.

And time has done his part and stands and looks
With dumb exasperated face. The books
Year after year record the crisis and
The passion, but no change. The measuring sand
    Is still. There are no flukes,

Like the virtuous sulphonamides, to kill
The poisons of the age, but only will:
Reduction of desires to that cold plan
Of raping the ideal; the new frail man
    Who slays what's in the hill.

The monkeys near the mess (where we all eat
And dream) I saw tonight select with neat
And brittle fingers dirty scraps, and fight,
And then look pensive in the fading light,
   And after pick their feet.

They are secured by straps about their slender
Waists, and the straps to chains. Most sad and tender,
They clasp each other and look round with eyes
Like ours at what their strange captivities
   Invisibly engender.

Today and Tomorrow

Tomorrow let us drive between the hills
And visit our good friends upon the farms,
Walking among the rows of sugar-cane
To look across their tassels at the snows.

And let us say good-day to sweet brown boys
Who keep their goats beneath that sheeted peak.
Tomorrow life will certainly be simple,
As at the drawing of an evening curtain.

Today there is the body to dispose of,
The blood to try to scour from all the house:
One must give lying smiles to calling neighbours
And soothe the children in the bedroom crying.

Today there is that terrible sense of guilt
And fear of being discovered; there is still
Regret for yesterday when everything
Was quiet and loving in tomorrow's way.

The Emotion of Fiction

Reading a book of tales
Which has stirred my imagination,
I have put down the book
And stared at the congregation
Of shadows and hollows which then
Made up the world; and found
Such meaning in meaningless things –
The neutral, patterned ground,
The figures on the sky –
As made me ache to tell
The single secret that runs,
Like a tendon, through it all.
And I could promise then
An overwhelming word,
A final revelation –
The image of a seabird
With scimitars of wings,
Pathetic feet tucked away,
A fine, ill-omened name,
Sweeping across the grey.
And I knew then the purpose
Of everything; that illusion
That comes in the unexpected
Moment, an aimed explosion.
Perhaps the object of art
Is this: the communication
Of that which cannot be told.
Worse: the rich explanation
That there is nothing to tell;
Only the artificial
Plot and ambiguous word,
The forged but sacred missal.
Even the word becomes
Merely a path to meaning;
It is the plot that stays
Longest, a model of leaning

Out over raging seas,
As if our ship or longing
Could weather infinite water
Or fatal, ghostly thronging.
If one could invent a plot
Whose action was slow as life
But vivid and absorbing,
With a last twist of the knife,
Virtues of furious neatness,
Coincidence, surprise,
The loves of the old or plain
Made plausible as lies.
And all to be ideal,
Even the gross and stupid
Details of passion and death
That one can never decide
Whether nothing or everything –
And then? Would that be more
Precise than this intense
But vague emotion? Roar,
Lions of living flesh,
On bone-strewed plains! It is
The winged and semi-human
Monsters of civilized myths
Whose terrible questions, above
Familiar evil or good,
Are unanswerable, but
Whose tongue is understood.

The Statue

The noises of the harbour die, the smoke is petrified
Against the thick but vacant, fading light, and shadows slide
From under stone and iron, darkest now. The last birds glide.

Upon this black-boned, white-splashed, far receding vista of grey
Is an equestrian statue, by the ocean, trampling the day,
Its green bronze flaked like petals, catching night before the bay.

Distilled from some sad, endless, sordid period of time,
As from the language of disease might come a consummate rhyme,
It tries to impose its values on the port and on the lime –

The droppings that by chance and from an uncontrollable
And savage life have formed a patina upon the skull;
Abandoned, have blurred a bodied vision once thought spare but
full –

On me, as authority recites to boys the names of queens.
Shall I be dazzled by the dynasties, the gules and greens,
The unbelievable art, and not recall their piteous means?

Last night I sailed upon that sea whose starting place is here,
Evaded the contraptions of the enemy, the mere
Dangers of water, saw the statue and the plinth appear.

Last night between the crowded, stifling decks I watched a man,
Smoking a big curved pipe, who contemplated his great wan
And dirty feet while minute after tedious minute ran –

This in the city now, whose floor is permanent and still,
Among the news of history and sense of an obscure will,
Is all the image I can summon up, my thought's rank kill;

As though there dominated this sea's threshold and this night
Not the raised hooves, the thick snake neck, the profile, and the
might,
The wrought, eternal bronze, the dead protagonist, the fight,

But that unmoving, pale but living shape that drops no tears,
Ridiculous and haunting, which each epoch reappears,
And is what history is not. O love, O human fears!

Epitaphs for Soldiers

I

Passing soldier stop and think
I was once as sad as you,
Saw in history a brink
More fearful than a bayonet's blue
– And left to what I thought but birds
The human message of these words.

II

Incredibly I lasted out a war,
Survived the unnatural, enormous danger
Of each enormous day. And so befell
A peril more enormous and still stranger:
The death by nature, chanceless, credible.

Winter in Camp

I

A three-badge killick in the public bar
Voluptuously sups his beer. The girl
Behind the counter reads an early *Star*.
Suddenly from the radio is a whirl
Of classical emotion, and the drums
Precisely mark despair, the violin
Unending ferment. Some chrysanthemums
Outside the window, yellow, pale, burn thin.

Not only these strange winter flowers take on
In this dread air the meaning of a myth,
But all the common objects now have gone
Into the littoral which borders death.
The ancient sailor holds an unplumbed glass;
The girl is instantly a sculptured mass.

II

The music and the shadows in the dark
Cinema stir a huge, authentic feeling,
And, when the lights come on, the shabby ceiling,
The scarred green walls and seats confirm the stark
Contrast between the crust and infinite deeps.
I go to the canteen, ramshackle, warm,
And move among the poor anonymous swarm;
I am awake but everybody sleeps.

Outside: the moonlit fields, the cruel blue –
Which box another world; as that absurd
Material life of sonneteers contains
A second, utterly unlike, self-made,
And contradicting all experience
Except this rarest, fearfullest, most true.

III

The trees I thought so cold and black and bare
In the late afternoon sprung softest browns:
The rain had stopped, and through the perspex air
The low sun made the land as green as downs.
The country hovered on a neutral edge;
And I was startled by a startled bird
Fluttering among the bayonets of the hedge –
And this is the illusion of the word.

Beyond the word, the chosen images,
Painful and moving as they are, I feel
Unutterably the epoch's tragedies,
Beside which this scene's cruelties are real
But hopelessly inadequate; like the pities
Of living airmen borne above smashed cities.

IV

What we imagined tortuously and dreaded
Comes like a friend advancing from the dark;
The morning sheet emphatically is leaded
With news of cities gone – and left unread.
And even as I write this, overhead,
The bombers fly to Europe. As I write:
In this bare camp, in country like a park,
Where uniforms and rain make thick the night.

Who now this winter dreads and who imagines?
The years of war pile on our heads like lime,
And horrors grow impersonal as engines;
Nor can I think in discipline and slime.
Perhaps beside some blue and neutral lake
Another Lenin sorts the real from fake.

V

Day after day upon the concrete square,
Cargo for sinking iron, sweaty places,
The men assemble with their cold, cramped faces,
Then go, for me forever, into air.
Their minds are full of images of fear,
Unending lust, their bodies in the traces
Of conformation: and the brief time races.
How will they recognize the crucial year?

Now man must be political or die;
Nor is there really that alternative.
Correctly to be dedicated and to live
By chance, is what the species asks. The sky
Is smutted with migrating birds or ships;
The kiss of winter is with cracking lips.

VI

And everywhere is that enormous lie;
So obvious that it seems to be the truth:
Like the first moment of a conjurer's failure,
Or visions of love from waves of cheap perfume
In villages on Sunday afternoons.
It even penetrates this quiet room,
Where three men round a stove are talking.
'The strikers should be shot,' one says: his hand
A craftsman's, capable and rough. The second:
'Niggers and Jews I hate.' It is the squawking
Of an obscene and guiltless bird. They sit,
Free men, in prison. And the third: 'I hate
Nobody' – raising, to gesticulate,
His arm in navy with a gun on it.

VII

Defined, undazzling, paper thin, the sun
At dusk: the moon at morning with the ghastly
Brightness of violet or mere decay.
And what, unconscious, we have truly done
Is done, and there remains the girl, the gun –
Embedded, actual, in the staring day
Night's symbols almost overwhelm us. Lastly:
The world which suffers of these things subtraction.

For what is now our life is neither dreams
Nor their more intricate and sensual stuff,
But that which to posterity descends
As formulae and measurements; which seems
To diggers, tombs, to critics, words; enough
To change the role of horses, hump waste sands.

VIII

What does the robin whisper and the trees,
Expressive of wind and winter, round this coast,
The human flesh that might contain a ghost?
Only plain words like *oil* and *manganese*.
It is not that our sensibilities
Are dead: what moved and frightened in the past
Confronts us still; still we construct the vast
Network of space from small realities.

But now the rotten crimson robes are falling,
What shaped them seen as bones with common names.
Magic is smothered under bribes, concessions:
Nothing beside the war can be appalling.
The victims of the sacrificial games
Discerned no symbolism in the lions.

IX

My working-party hacks the grass, the tall
Tubers of summer rusty as the sickle.
In camp a season, these young men have all
A respite from the battle over nickel
– Or dynasties or rubber, anything
But what is mass-induced into their heads.
And while they work they sentimentally sing:
As credulously they will go to beds
As graves.

        Their weakness is the measure of
My own; their guilt my own inactive past;
Their stormy future mine, who wish that love
Could melt the guns, expropriate a caste.
How, when my only rank is consciousness,
Can I despise them, far less pity, bless?

2

———

1945–1962

During a Bombardment by V-Weapons

The little noises of the house:
Drippings between the slates and ceiling;
From the electric fire's cooling,
Tickings; the dry feet of a mouse:

These at the ending of a war
Have power to alarm me more
Than the ridiculous detonations
Outside the gently coughing curtains.

And, love, I see your pallor bears
A far more pointed threat than steel.
Now all the permanent and real
Furies are settling in upstairs.

Schwere Gustav

Schwere Gustav, built by Krupps,
Was the largest of all guns:
Of thirty-one-inch calibre,
It fired a shell of seven tons.

Worked by fifteen hundred troops
Topped by a general, no less,
Gustav fired two rounds a day,
But after sixty was u/s.

The soldiers seeing Gustav's barrel
Huge against the eastern sky,
And his complicated breech,
Knew why they had got to die.

Accumulated capital
Made possible this symbol of
Our deep, ridiculous desires.
O war, O Gustav and O love!

Meditation

Now the ambassadors have gone, refusing
Our gifts, treaties, anger, compliance;
And in their place the winter has arrived,
Icing the culture-bearing water.
We brood in our respective empires on
The words we might have said which would have breached
The Chinese wall round our superfluous love
And manufactures. We do not brood too deeply.
There are our friends' perpetual, subtle demands
For understanding: visits to those who claim
To show us what is meant by death,
And therefore life, our short and puzzling lives,
And to explain our feelings when we look
Through the dark sky to other lighted worlds –
The well-shaved owners of sanatoria,
And raving, grubby oracles: the books
On diet, posture, prayer and aspirin art:
The claims of frightful weapons to be investigated:
Mad generals to be promoted: and
Our private gulfs to slither down in bed.
Perhaps in spring the ambassadors will return.
Before then we shall find perhaps that bombs,
Books, people, planets, worry, even our wives,
Are not at all important. Perhaps
The preposterous fishing-line tangle of undesired
Human existence will suddenly unravel
Before some staggering equation
Or mystic experience, and God be released
From the moral particle or blue-lit room.
Or, better still, perhaps we shall, before
Anything really happens, be safely dead.

To My Son

When you can understand
This endless paper that I cover,
With what strange feeling will you find
That I feared and loved, was sensitive, not clever.

For it's to you I write
(My only true posterity)
This verse that seems not to better what
I seized from environment and ancestry.

I should not mind your smile
At all the crudities and gaps –
By that less likely yourself to fail
To raise up character and living's lapse.

Critic and art in one;
Not tied by fate and yet unfree;
The classic killer, loving son;
Yes, you'll know each word I add is irony.

From Epitaphs + Occasions 1949

The Gaze

Catching myself obliquely in the glass,
I thought I saw my father.
He died at my age now, but the years that pass
Do not destroy him – rather
Make him resume his dense forgotten mass.

From Epitaphs + Occasions 1949

Although the memory of his face has gone
I know mine different,
And what I see in mirrors is the wan
Dwarf that the orbit bent –
The Dog-star's mysterious companion.

How well I understand what he transmitted!
The gaze that travelling
At will through the generations sees the pitted
Mask of the timeless thing,
And knows itself both weak and dedicated.

Obituary of R. Fuller

We note the death, with small regret,
Of one who'd scarcely lived, as yet.
Born just before the First World War,
Died when there'd only been one more:
Between, his life had all been spent
In the small-bourgeois element,
Sheltered from poverty and hurt,
From passion, tragedy and dirt.
His infant traumas somewhat worse,
He would have written better verse,
His youth by prudence not so guided
His politics been more decided.
In the event his life was split
And half was lost bewailing it:
Part managerial, part poetic –
Hard to decide the more pathetic.
Avoiding China, Spain and Greece,
He passed his adult years of peace
In safe unease, with thoughts of doom
(As birth is feared inside the womb) –
Doom of his talent and his place,
Doom, total, of the human race.
This strange concern for fellow creatures
Had certainly some pathic features.
He could not understand that death
Must be the lot of all with breath,
And crudely linked felicity
With dying from senile decay,
Finding no spiritual worth

In guided missiles, torture, dearth.
Quite often he was heard to babble
'Poets should be intelligible'
Or 'What determines human fate
Is the class structure of the state'
Or 'Freud and Marx and Dickens found –
And so do I – souls not profound'.
These views were logically a feature
Of his rude, egotistic nature –
So unemotional and shy
Such friends as he retained would cry
With baffled boredom, thankful they
Were not part of his family.

If any bit of him survives
It will be that verse which contrives
To speak in private symbols for
The peaceful caught in public war.
For there his wavering faith in man
Wavers around some sort of plan,
And though foreseeing years of trouble,
Denies a universal rubble,
Discovering in wog and sailor
The presages of bourgeois failure.
Whether at this we weep or laugh
It makes a generous epitaph.

Rhetoric of a Journey

The train takes me away from the northern valleys
Where I lived my youth and where my youth lives on
In the person of my parent and the stone walls,
The dialect of love I understand
But scarcely speak, the mills and illnesses.

In Trollope's novel open on my knee
The characters are worried about money:

The action revolves round the right to a necklace.
I have only to bend my head and immediately
I am lost in this other reality, the world
Of art, where something is always missing.
In *The Eustace Diamonds* life is made tolerable
By standing away from time and refusing to write
Of the hours that link the official biography.

I think of the poem I wrote on another visit –
A list of the poet's hoarded perceptions:
The net of walls thrown over waves of green,
The valleys clogged with villages, the cattle
Pink against smoking mills – and only now
Experience what was delayed and omitted.
For those were rooms in which we dared not look
At each other's load of emotion: it was there
Our past had to die: and where we acknowledged
With pain and surprise our ties with the disregarded.
I would like to renounce the waking rational life,
The neat completed work, as being quite
Absurd and cowardly; and leave to posterity
The words on book-marks, enigmatic notes,
Thoughts before sleep, the vague unwritten verse
On people, on the city to which I travel.
I would like to resolve to live fully
In the barbarous world of sympathy and fear.

Says his life to the poet: 'Can you make verse of this?'
And the poet answers: 'Yes, it is your limitations
That enable me to get you down at all.'
The diamonds glitter on his paper and
His sons sail unloved to the Antipodes.
Those whom a lack of creativeness condemns
To truth see magazines in the hands of the patient
And realize that the serial will go on
After death; but the artist becomes ill himself.
For only the fully-committed participate
In the revolution of living, the coming to power
Of death: the others have always some excuse

To be absent from the shooting, to be at home
Curled up with a book or at the dentist's.

Sometimes I find it possible to feign
The accent of the past, the vulgar speech
Which snobbery and art have iced; but feel no longer
The compulsion of hills, the eternal interests
Which made my fathers understand each other.
That mockery of solidarity
Some of the civilized always experience,
Waiting half hopefully for the dreaded barbarians,
Sick of their culture, traitors to the division
Of toil and sensibility. Yet really
I can speak easily only to myself.
The tears meant for others are wept in front of the glass;
The confession is never posted; and the eye
Slides away from the proffered hand and discovers
An interesting view from the window.

The ridiculous mottled faces pass in stiff
Procession: relations, friends and chance encounters.
And the asinine minds that lie behind the gestures
Of goodness I can never reciprocate
Repel me with their inability
To escape from the grossest errors. Is it weakness
That sometimes imagines these shaped as heroes?
That cannot conceive of happiness as other
Than the apotheosis of the simple and kind?
That refuses to see how the century rises, pale,
From the death of its dream, ignoring the gains
Of the cruel, the different wishes of slaves?

The train removes me to another set
Of evasions. The valleys disappear. The train
Bolts through the central plain. I shall discover
Whether Lizzie Eustace retained her diamonds,
How far the hordes are from the city,
And my end will make significant for me
A casual place and date. My own child

Will grow from the generous warmth of his youth and perhaps
Discover, like me, that the solemn moments of life
Require their unbearable gaucheness translated to art.
For the guilt of being alive must be appeased
By the telling observation, and even feeling
Can only be borne retrospectively.
Bending over to kiss, the sensitive see with alarm
That their selves are still upright: the instant of death is announced
By a rattle of tin in the corridor. Meaning is given
These disparate happenings, our love is only
Revealed, by conventions: 'Dear Mother, I hope you are better.'
Or 'Lizzie resolved that she would have her revenge.'
The lilac will last a fortnight if the rain
Arrives, the sparrows will always turn to let
Their lime drop over the gutter, the gardener
Will lift the chickweed, and the clots of nests
In the elms disappear in the whirling green of summer.

At the end of the twilit road a figure is standing
Calling us to go in, while the far-off rumours
Of terrible facts which at last may destroy
Our happiness spoil our play. In the place we go to
The kettle boils on the fire, the brasses are polished,
But people are busy with pain in another room.
One night I shall watch the city and black sky meet
In the distance, the car lights stream on the heath like tracer,
And in such moments of lonely and mild exultation
This rhetoric will be forgotten, and the life of omission go on.
Behind me will lie the sad and convulsive events
As narrative art, and as fated, immortal and false.

Youth Revisited

The hastening cloud grows thin; the sun's pale disc
Swells, haloes, then bursts out and warms the stone,
Pitching the yew's black tent on brilliant green.
A dozen years have gone since last I saw
This tiny church set on the parkland's edge
Between the glistening hunters and the cattle,
A Sunday exercise for week-end guests,
And I approach it conscious that emotion
Ought to be suffered, as indeed it is.
Did I live here and was I happy then?
A war more innocent, an age of man
Removed, my poems thick with formal doom
And baseless faith in humans. Years that now
Pass with the clarity of hours then
Record the degeneration of the nerves
And the world situation, make a golden
Time from that decade of infirm belief.

I am half glad to find the place has marked
Dramatically my absence. All the roof
Has gone, grass flutters on the broken stone,
A notice says *These walls are dangerous.*
Through unglazed windows marble monuments
Are glimpsed like modest spinsters in their baths.
Bombs or neglect, informants are not sure:
In any case the church will now decay
With other luxuries. The horses are
Not here, no doubt the mansion house beyond
The lake is requisitioned by the state,
And furrows creep across the pleasure ground.

I wonder if my son completely fails
To grasp my halting reconstruction of
My youth. Here, where we brought him in our arms
Was neat then, facing time with fortitude.
The statues in the gloom stood for their moral,

The wicked viscount's smoke rose from the house,
The evils of the epoch had not quite
Made rational the artist's accidie.

And yet, the clock moved on another twelve,
He would have something still to put to his son.
The jet planes slither overhead, a frog
Throbs in the dust half-way across the road,
Over two fields a saw scrapes like a bird.
Creatures, machines and men live yet among
The partial, touching ruins of their world.

The Image

A spider in the bath. The image noted:
Significant maybe but surely cryptic.
A creature motionless and rather bloated,
The barriers shining, vertical and white:
Passing concern, and pity mixed with spite.

Next day with some surprise one finds it there.
It seems to have moved an inch or two, perhaps.
It starts to take on that familiar air
Of prisoners for whom time is erratic:
The filthy aunt forgotten in the attic.

Quite obviously it came up through the waste,
Rejects through ignorance or apathy
That passage back. The problem must be faced;
And life go on though strange intruders stir
Among its ordinary furniture.

One jibs at murder, so a sheet of paper
Is slipping beneath the accommodating legs.
The bathroom window shows for the escaper
The lighted lanterns of laburnum hung
In copper beeches – on which scene it's flung.

We certainly would like thus easily
To cast out of the house all suffering things.
But sadness and responsibility
For our own kind lives in the image noted:
A half-loved creature, motionless and bloated.

Translation

Now that the barbarians have got as far as Picra,
And all the new music is written in the twelve-tone scale,
And I am anyway approaching my fortieth birthday,
    I will dissemble no longer.

I will stop expressing my belief in the rosy
Future of man, and accept the evidence
Of a couple of wretched wars and innumerable
    Abortive revolutions.

I will cease to blame the stupidity of the slaves
Upon their masters and nurture, and will say,
Plainly, that they are enemies to culture,
    Advancement and cleanliness.

From progressive organizations, from quarterlies
Devoted to daring verse, from membership of
Committees, from letters of various protest
    I shall withdraw forthwith.

When they call me reactionary I shall smile,
Secure in another dimension. When they say
'Cinna has ceased to matter' I shall know
    How well I reflect the times.

The ruling class will think I am on their side
And make friendly overtures, but I shall retire
To the side farther from Picra and write some poems
    About the doom of the whole boiling.

[handwritten marginal note: From Counterparts 1954]

Anyone happy in this age and place
    Is daft or corrupt. Better to abdicate
From a material and spiritual terrain
        Fit only for barbarians.

The Meeting

At the ineffective meeting is received
    The letter: 'From your guilt
I resign. I exculpate myself from all
        Your pistols and libels.

'I shall devote myself henceforth to God
    And the investigation of freedom.
I write from a country cottage where the chestnut
        Makes miniature

'Images of itself with its sea-scum blossom.
    Your world is urban and evil.
My cat advises me: remove my name, please,
        From your list of dog-lovers.'

The committee composes its reply: 'We, too,
    Have seen that tree in spring
Making pink blotting paper of the lawns.
        And as for the shootings

'They were of those who would have let art die
    With lovely anaemia.
Your cat is right: his name has been embossed
        On our notepaper.

'Consider: we need your support who are able even
    To formulate the questions.
Try to recover the original impulse
        That led you to join us.

'For the season now is nearly over and
    The orators put away
Their stools. The belting slows. The tubes are about
        To leap from their racks.'

Autobiography of a Lungworm

My normal dwelling is the lungs of swine,
    My normal shape a worm,
But other dwellings, other shapes, are mine
    Within my natural term.
Dimly I see my life, of all, the sign,
    Of better lives the germ.

The pig, though I am inoffensive, coughs,
    Finding me irritant:
My eggs go with the contents of the troughs
    From mouth to excrement –
The pig thus thinks, perhaps, he forever doffs
    His niggling resident.

The eggs lie unconsidered in the dung
    Upon the farmyard floor,
Far from the scarlet and sustaining lung:
    But happily a poor
And humble denizen provides a rung
    To make ascension sure.

The earthworm eats the eggs; inside the warm
    Cylinder larvae hatch:
For years, if necessary, in this form
    I wait the lucky match
That will return me to my cherished norm,
    My ugly pelt dispatch.

Strangely, it is the pig himself becomes
    The god inside the car:

His greed devours the earthworms; so the slums
    Of his intestines are
The setting for the act when clay succumbs
    And force steers for its star.

The larvae burrow through the bowel wall
    And, having to the dregs
Drained ignominy, gain the lung's great hall.
    They change. Once more, like pegs,
Lungworms are anchored to the rise and fall
    – And start to lay their eggs.

What does this mean? The individual,
    Nature, mutation, strife?
I feel, though I am simple, still the whole
    Is complex; and that life –
A huge, doomed throbbing – has a wiry soul
    That must escape the knife.

On Grazing a Finger

In time and place such wounds are staggered;
Healing, too, holds them in dominion.
I am most thankful under the surface
A ghastly thing moves on its skeleton.

The Day

At the time it seemed unimportant: he was lying
In bed, off work, with a sudden pain,
And she was haloed by the morning sun,
Enquiring if he'd like the daily paper.

So idle Byzantium scarcely felt at first
The presence in her remoter provinces
Of the destructive followers of the Crescent.
But in retrospect that day of moderate health
Stood fired in solid and delightful hues,
The last of joy, the first of something else –
An inconceivable time when sex could be
Grasped for the asking with gigantic limbs,
When interest still was keen in the disasters
Of others – accident, uprising, drouth –
And the sharp mind perceived the poignancy
Of the ridiculous thoughts of dissolution.

A day remembered by a shrivelled empire
Nursed by hermaphrodites and unsustained
By tepid fluids poured in its crying mouth.

The Ides of March

Fireballs and thunder augment the wailing wind:
A vulgar score, but not inappropriate
To my romantic, classic situation.
Within the house my wife is asleep and dreaming
That I, too, am cocooned inside the world
Of love whose fear is that the other world
Will end it. But I wait uneasy here
Under the creaking trees, the low dark sky,
For the conspirators. This is the place
Where I come, in better weather, with a book
Or pen and paper – for I must confess
To a little amateur scribbling. Love and letters:
One ought to be content – would, if the times
Were different; if state and man were free,
The slaves fed well, and wars hung over us
Not with death's certainty but with the odds
Merely of dying a not too painful death.
Yes, I have caught the times like a disease

Whose remedy is still experimental;
And felt the times as some enormous gaffe
I cannot forget. And now I am about
To cease being a fellow traveller, about
To select from several complex panaceas,
Like a shy man confronted with a box
Of chocolates, the plainest after all.
I am aware that in my conscious wish
To rid the empire of a tyrant there
Is something that will give me personal pleasure;
That usually one's father's death occurs
About the time one becomes oneself a father.
These subtleties are not, I think, important –
No more than that I shall become a traitor,
Technically, to my class, my friend, my country.
No, the important thing is to remove
Guilt from this orchard, which is why I have
Invited here those men of action with
Their simpler motives and their naked knives.
I hope my wife will walk out of the house
While I am in their compromising presence,
And know that what we built had no foundation
Other than luck and my false privileged rôle
In a society that I despised.
And then society itself, aghast,
Reeling against the statue, also will
Be shocked to think I had a secret passion.
Though passion is, of course, not quite the word:
I merely choose what history foretells.
The dawn comes moonlike now between the trees
And silhouettes some rather muffled figures.
It is embarrassing to find oneself
Involved in this clumsy masquerade. There still
Is time to send a servant with a message:
'Brutus is not at home': time to postpone
Relief and fear. Yet, plucking nervously
The pregnant twigs, I stay. Good morning, comrades.

The Perturbations of Uranus

Such fame as I have drops from me in a flash
When the girl behind the café bar sends back
A candid gaze. I judge her by the lack
Of overt imperfections in her flesh
And by her youth, but fear she will advance
Such standards to me. I open my book and read
That the sole sin is human ignorance,
Through mind must stretch the future of the breed.

I agree, without reservations I agree;
But glance occasionally where the urn
Distorts the image of her whom I confirm
Is not distorted, and again I see
How still the world belongs to the obtuse
And passionate, and that the bosom's small
But noticeable curve subtends its tall
Explosions and orations of mad abuse.

A fraud, then, this concern about the fate
Of the supposedly less rational?
No, but the powers that dissuade from all
Libidinous action rise from our weakest part.
And I go out into the urban grey,
Where one vermilion bus sign hangs as though
Placed by a careful painter, and array
Again my lust with the armour of outward show.

The planet Neptune's existence was revealed
Only by the perturbations of Uranus.
Crabbed lines of poetry, pigments congealed
Insanely on a little canvas train us
For those transcendent moments of existence
In which the will is powerless, and the blind
Astonished flesh forgets that it is kind
And drives in love or murder with its pistons.

Our art is the expression of desire,
Yeats said; and one who buys a landscape for
Its beauty takes home in his arms the bare
Outrageousness of an uncaring whore –
Among this trivial brick such rhetoric seems
Irrelevant to the short degraded lives
For whom the artist plans, the prophet dreams,
Perversely, virtuous law and golden hives.

Girl, through young generations still unborn
You will induce again and yet again
Disturbances within the learned men;
And they will feel brain from spare body torn,
Whether they hear, in ruins that their pity
Failed to prevent, their fear knew they would meet,
Or in the intact and reasonable city,
The disrespectful giggles of the street.

Mythological Sonnets

To my son

I

Far out, the voyagers clove the lovat sea
Which fizzed a little round its oily calms,
Straw sun and bleached planks swinging, the
Gunwale ribbed with a score of tawny arms.
Nursing a bellyache, a rope-rubbed hand
Or a vague passion for the cabin boy,
Accustomed to the rarity of land
And water's ennui, these found all their joy
In seeing the hyphens of archipelagos
Or a green snake of coast rise and fall back.
And little they imagined that in those
Inlets and groves, stretched out as on the rack,
Their girls were ground under the enormous thews
Of visiting gods, watched by staid munching ewes.

II

There actually stood the fabled riders,
Their faces, to be truthful, far from white;
Their tongue incomprehensible, their height
Negligible: in a word, complete outsiders.

Why had they come? To wonder at the tarts,
Trade smelly hides, gawp at the statuary,
Copy our straddling posture and our arts?
How right that we had not thought fit to flee!

'Join us at cocktails, bathing?' No reply.
'Let's see your wild dances, hear your simple airs.'
No move save the shifting of a shifty eye.

Trailing great pizzles, their dun stallions
Huddled against the hedges while our mares
Cavorted on the grass, black, yellow, bronze.

III

The legendary woman he had sought,
Whose name had been as threadbare and remote
As God's, whose awful loveliness was taught
With participle, peak and asymptote,

Now lay below him smiling past his gaze;
The breasts a little flaccid on their cage
Of ribs, her belly's skin as speckled as
A flower's throat. She had been caught by age.

And he could see that even in the past
The pillars that enclosed the myth concealed
A slippery stinking altar and a vast
Horde of lewd priests to whom all was revealed.

Yet she was fair still, and he cried out in vain
To reach and own her far complacent fane.

IV

Beneath a bit of dirty cloth a girl's
Thin severed hand; a portrait of a man
Streaming with blood from badly painted curls;
A withered heart just pulsing in a pan.

Even though these have been displayed to us
Can we believe them or the cause of their
Existence, comically anomalous?
Here under peeling walls, a sceptic stare,

The hand writes its seditious words of love,
Belief goes on being painfully expressed,
And pity flutters at its far remove
From the historical tormented breast.

Did God intend this squalid spuriousness
To mean both what it is and purports? Yes.

V

A granulated, storm-blown, ashen sky
Behind blanched, still unruined columns where
Monarch and queen, prophetic sister, dry
Old statesman still descend a marble stair.

'You are my destiny.' 'Do not go forth
Today in combat.' 'This whole realm is sick.'
Their voices rise into the breaking light
And die away towards the barbarous north.

These could not, though half conscious of their plight,
Grasp the extent of time's appalling trick
That stole the flesh that was so sweet and thick,
Broke wall and bones, saved from the gorgeous site
Some kitchen pot, discarded and obese,
And gave the great names to horses and disease.

VI

The sage cut an orange through the navel, dwelt
Upon the curious pattern then revealed.
Breaking a habit makes the world, he felt,
Burst out with meanings usually concealed.

Experimenting later with that girl
Who cooked his rice and dusted all his books,
He saw what he had never seen – a curl
Soft in the well where the neck's sinews rise;
And yearned in pity that with no rebuke
She lent herself to these perverted grips.

But as for her, she never thought her lot
Called for emotion. This strange exercise
Came with the rice and dust – the habitual cut
Of a world small and dry and full of pips.

VII

Well now, the virgin and the unicorn –
Although its point and details are obscure
The theme speeds up the pulses, to be sure.
No doubt it is the thought of that long horn
Inclined towards a lady young, well-born,
Unfearful, naïve, soft, ecstatic, pure.
How often, dreaming, have we found the cure
For our malaise, to tear or to be torn!

In fact, the beast and virgin merely sat,
I seem to think, in some enamelled field;
He milky, muscular, and she complete
In kirtle, bodice, wimple. Even that
Tame conjugation makes our eyeballs yield
Those gems we long to cast at someone's feet.

VIII

Suns in a skein, the uncut stones of night,
Calm planets rising, violet, golden, red –
Bear names evolved from man's enormous head
Of gods who govern battle, rivers, flight,
And goddesses of science and delight;
Arranged in the mortal shapes of those who bled
To found a dynasty or in great dread
Slept with their destiny, full-breasted, white.

But long before stout Venus, clanking Mars,
What appellations had the eternal stars?
When, cheek by jowl with burial pits, rank dens
Lay open to the dark, and dwarfish men
Stared under huge brow-ridges, wits awry,
What fearful monsters slouched about the sky?

IX

Naked, the girl repelled his lustful hands:
Her shining skin exuded awe, like art.
The visiting god held out his simple gift
And, stepping modestly across the sands,
The innocent fool played her predestined part
And clad herself in the lubricious shift.

Years later and from that same place their child,
Lugging his vessel to the sheltered reach,
Started on his heroic bloody fate.
The ancient motive of his father bent
His gaze towards the ocean, wine-dark, wild:
He never saw upon the trampled beach
The thing that had assumed, but all too late,
The hard epidermis of a succulent.

X

Girls fight like fiends in paintings to defend
Themselves from centaurs: envious, outraged,
We never think (our feelings too engaged)
The crisis through to its surprising end
When the sad, baffled beast with clumsy hooves
Paws impotently at the delicate
And now relenting limbs. So Hercules,
Whose lovely wife the centaur Nessus got,
Should not have loosed at him the angry shot
That stained the shirt that brought the hero's fate.

I do not know what this conclusion proves
Unless it is that honest lust will freeze
To piteous art, and subtle jealousy
Must poison needlessly what has to be.

XI

Mysterious indeed are epochs, dates
And influences: how a woman springs
Into a painting of organic things
And gradually moves forward till the great
Shoulders and flanks blot out the foliate
Sepia. Then once more the fashion swings:
Among a tempted saint's imaginings
A thin pot-bellied virgin emanates.

Even the most serene and opulent
Goddesses rise from the sordid life of man,
Who catching, say, a girl in stockinged feet
Arranging a shop-window sees the event
Translated to a new and staggering span
Of art, the previous pantheon obsolete.

XII

That the dread happenings of myths reveal
Our minds' disorder is a commonplace.
Myths, too, are history's half-forgotten face
Remoulded by desire, though we will feel
Compared with myths contemporary life unreal.
Tower and wall may sink without a trace
But the strong sense of lust and of disgrace
Lives on.
        Ourselves have seen Prometheus steal
The fire the overlords denied to man,
Which act enchained him to Caucasian rocks.
We still await the hero that must free
The great conception whose ambiguous plan
At once brought to the world its evil box
And the sole chance to share felicity.

XIII

Once brought indoors the leaf-eyed cat became
An emblem disproportionately odd.
Its blunt head, much enlarged but looking tame,
Displaced the human lineaments of God.
The teasing beast that squatted on her rock
And ate the duffers had a feline face,
And even he who turned the riddle's lock
Went on to symbolize mankind's disgrace.

Down corridors of night an awful thing
Brushes against us softly like a wing.
Our hands that reach across the bed for her
We love meet unexpected, frightening fur.
And looking in the glass we find at last
The claw-made lacerations of the past.

XIV

Discovered in this vine-ridged, rounded land
In which its tutelary goddess, tanned
And huge, had spent her slender mortal youth –
A number of ancient men. Old age, old age!
Wine, evening sunshine, philosophic truth –
Nothing can still that agonizing rage
For what was never ruled but for an hour
And now lies far beyond the sceptre's power.

Towards the temple stride young girls whose dress,
Taut with the zephyr of their passage, shows
The secret lack which men initially
Despise, then eye with tragic covetousness,
And lastly envy, conscious of the blows
Time hammers on their superfluity.

XV

Even (we think) the heroes cracked at last –
Great lumping extroverts with shields that pelts
Of only fabulous beasts could cover, vast
Lickerishness and canyons of half-healed welts.

The man of ordinary valour, size,
Finds it impossible to visualize
These others – who had been alone with girls
On islands, with their deeds like daydreams, curls,

Hawk profiles, iron paps – that these could creep
Far from the friendly tents, the invading hordes,
And throw themselves upon the ground and weep
Or, growing mad, attempt to eat their swords.

Such were the flaws their sires could not foresee,
Blinded by marvellous human nudity.

XVI

How startling to find the portraits of the gods
Resemble men! Even those parts where we
Might have expected to receive the odds
Are very modest, perhaps suspiciously.

For we cannot forget that these aloof and splendid
Figures with negligible yards and curls
Arranged in formal rising suns descended,
With raging lust, on our astonished girls –

No doubt because they were intimidated
By their own kind (those perfect forms that man,
Ironically, has always adulated)
And craved the extravagance of nature's plan.

So that humanity's irregular charms
In time fused with divine breasts, buttocks, arms.

XVII

We read of children taken by the heel
And tossed over battlements; a sharp hot stake
Sizzling in a giant's eye; and near a lake
Two tender virgins lying naked while
Unknown to them four indescribable
Monsters approach. That world, we much would like
To think, is simply an artistic fake,
Nothing to do with that in which we dwell.

But could mere images make even now
Ears drum with lust, the chest run secret shame?
The myths are here: it was our father's name
The maiden shrieked in horror as she turned
To wrinkled bark; our dearest flesh that burned,
Straddling her legs inside the wooden cow.

XVIII

The stench hung even in the garden: down
The corridor it thickened: in the room
It strangled us. The visage, cramped and brown,
Seemed to belong already in the tomb.

'How long has he been at this dreadful point?'
– Idle remark to try to hide our fears;
But the astonishing reply was: 'Years.'

And as the sheet was lifted to anoint
The noisome wound we shudderingly turned
And tried to understand what we had learned:

That this old squalid hurt was done some bright
Day when it seemed there was no end to truth,
And the large heroes wandered in the sight
Of gods still faithful, through the planet's youth.

XIX

Stone countenances, bearded, ill with time;
The screeching class of starlings, dissident,
In cultured cities; crooked wigs of lime
That contradict the famous masks' intent –
The nervous images that haunt an age
Bud in the unremembered past and flower
In that long battle art and history wage:
And epochs compressed in childhood and the womb
Breed the regalia of the public hour.
The murdered father's head leans by those doors;
The brothers' quarrel stands behind the doom
Of one life's sickening and recurrent wars;
And the smooth tongue that offers love is built
On teeth ground flat in violent dreams of guilt.

Monologue in Autumn

With yellow teeth the hunter tears and crunches
Whole boughs of the quince, then walks away,
His hind legs on a mannequin's straight line.
The clipped back (ample as a bed, unyielding
Save for a slight threat like an anchored ship)
Returns what always astonishes – the warmth
Of a new embrace.
                                    And you arrive. I help
To raise your body in its carapace
Of steel and leather. Then I see you move,
A centaur, down the slopes towards the plain
Where in the mist the sun already hangs
Its monstrous copper and autumnal shape.

You fade. I turn across the leaf-crumbed lawn:
Under the mulberry the gales have torn
A cat gnaws the purple lining of the pelt
It emptied yesterday.
                                    And now the house:
First the twin balustrades and then the busts
Whose formal curls and noses are as rough
As if their existence truly were marine
Under the window's random lights. Inside,
The books propound what all books must propound:
Whether man shall accept the authority of God
Or of his senses.
                                    In the drawing room
The fire sadly burns for no one: soon
Your guests will descend, taste tea on Sunday tongues;
Their lives and mine and yours go on with talk,
The disposition of chairs and lamps, the opened
Doors to the terrace, the order of good-nights.

Hard to imagine that the ambassador,
Your cousin, lives at this same hour among
Furs, fuming breaths, ardours of moral striving;

That such half world exists for which our own
Has manufactured all its cruel swords and faces
Whose profits surround us here as love affairs,
Portable sketching outfits, hair arranged
Like savages and scented with the whole
Resources of science.
                              Yet this must account
For what I feel, in love with you, within
This house and season – that residual sadness
After bare rooms and trees have been subtracted
And love has learned the trick of suffering
Its object's relative indifference.
Why, as you always ask, should I so dread
What threatens from the rivalry of two
Crude ways of life, two grotesque empires, whose
Ideals, diplomacy and soldiery
We must despise? But merely to formulate
The question seems to me to answer it,
And show that shameful collective death as quite
Other than what we think of in the dawn –
The torturer that will test us in our cell.

I open the piano, sound a note,
Remember dreams. How could you come to grow
In my imagination (that must have been
My wish) so sallow and in such a place –
As strange and circumstantial as the future?
You said the words too wild to be recalled,
Lay back and gently died.
                              You will return,
Your horse not sweating quite enough to mark
The lapse of time. I shall forbear to ask
The question that makes pain a certainty,
But merely look with the avoiding eyes
Of a Cesario or Cordelia.

And dinner will stretch into drowsiness,
Owls swing like theatre fairies past the moon
Whose battered lantern lights the tops of woods

And shines along the calm, dividing sea,
Painting with fire the armour in the harbours
Which lie encircled by their snowy lands
And multiplicity of helpless wills.
The uninvited images invade
The separate and sleeping heads: dead branches
Threading the sockets of those equine skulls
Whose riders perished in the useless war,
Whose teeth are rattled in their open jaws
By tempests from sastrugi, and whose foals
Stream through what whitens their brazil-nut eyes
Towards savannahs where the planet holds
Only inhuman species to its pap.

On the Mountain

I

Why red, why red? I ask myself, observing
A girl's enamelled nails, not understanding
The convention – an unrealistic art.

I live in a suburb of the capital,
A hill of villas, and sometimes note such things;
Old enough to remember better days.

The stoics have virtually disappeared.
I like to think myself the last of them,
Shaken but not devoured by ghastly omens.

The theatres are given up to leg shows
And gladiatorial games. The savage beasts
Are weary with the number of their victims.

In poetry the last trace of conviction
Has long since been extinguished. Round the temples
Are crowds of flautists, eunuchs and raving females.

The decoration of the baths and other
Edifices of importance is assigned
To those same careless slaves who mix the mortar.

The so-called educated classes share
The superstitions and amusements of
The vulgar, gawping at guts and moaning singers.

Atrocious taxes to 'defend' the frontiers;
Fixing maximum prices yet deploring the black market
– These the preoccupations of the state.

And the alarming aspect of imperial
Succession! The imperial madness! O
My country, how long shall we bear such things?

I find a little comfort in recalling
That complaints of evil times are found in every
Age which has left a literature behind:

And that the lyric is always capable
Of rejuvenation (as is the human heart),
Even in times of general wretchedness.

II

In my garden, at the risk of annoying my cat,
I rescue a fledgling: as it squeaks, I see
That its tongue is like something inside a watch.

They would not find it odd, those Others –
Mysterious community, not outside
And not within the borders of the empire;

Not the barbarians precisely nor
The slaves: indeed, from their strange treason no
Mind is exempt … even the emperor's!

Could I believe? Surrender to the future,
The inevitability of the future – which
Nevertheless can only come by martyrdom?

Respect those priestly leaders, arguing
Whether the Second Person of the Three
Is equal or subordinate to the First?

While in their guarded monasteries they lift
Their greasy cassocks to ecstatic girls –
Under the bed their secret box of coin.

I suppose their creed must conquer in the end
Because it gives the simplest and most complete
Answer to all men ask in these bad years.

Is there a life beyond this life? Must art
Be the maidservant of morality?
And will the humble triumph? Yes. Yes. Yes.

Disgusting questions, horrible reply;
Deplorable the course of history:
And yet we cannot but regard with awe

The struggle of the locked and rival systems,
Involving the entire geography
Of the known world, through epochs staggeringly prolonged.

To name our cities after poets, or
To hasten the destruction of the species –
The debate continues chronic and unresolved.

III

How rapidly one's thoughts get out of hand!
With my unsatisfactory physique
I watch the blossom through the blinding rain,

Cringe the while at the shoddy workmanship
Of the piddling gutter – typical of the times –
And stroke with skeleton hand the mortal fur.

It is as hard to realize where we are
As for the climber on the famous peak
For whom the familiar outline is no more

The record of a deadly illness or
The tearing organs of a bird of prey
But merely boredom, breathing, prudence, stones.

from *Faustian Sketches*

Questions to Mephistopheles

I

'Why did I choose this trivial shape,' you ask –
'The rouge, the plumpness and the mincing gait?'
I answer: is it not appropriate
For one whose Master laid on him the task

Of undertaking that the Paphian flask
And the Circassian dancing girl await
The soul's vendor? Besides, one can't equate
The real me with any human mask.

I mean, think how God's hate must change the entire
Expression, serving Satan hump the back;
Imagine further how the holocaust
Of hell dries up the flesh, that devils lack,
Like angels, sex and therefore must perspire
In vile self-love. Perhaps imagine Faust.

II

'If Mephistopheles in serving Faust
Can bring on dancing girls and get him soused
Why doesn't Mephistopheles thus serve
Himself?' It's not that I haven't got the nerve,
And obviously not because I think
There's any turpitude in sex and drink.

Why then? Remember that my former state
Was perfect innocence, without desire
Except to praise my God. Then came the dire
Notion He fell in love with to create
A being of moral cowardice and great
Pudenda. From that time His angel choir
– Thirst still unknown to them, groins still entire –
Were set to shaping man's disgusting fate.

The Princes

A reckless use of fur and cloth of gold,
Wastage of peacocks, boars and apple fool,
Enormous men with hired tights and pig
Eyes who surround descending princes,
Bargaining at impossible hours amid
Small tipsy trebles and Mongolian
Acrobats – this is how fate is ordered through
The world's inhabited and cultured regions.

At such a weighty congress Faust arrives –
Another wizard (though a famous one)
Among decipherers and economists
And experts in the ailments of old men.
Having passed all his life through want and wars,
Innumerable wrong decisions, tyrannies,
And bluff field-marshals, he has always dreamed
Of finding a second youth and reckless power.

Two or three kings are playing in the garden
With variable skill at cup and ball.
'Peru, this is the celebrated Faust ...'
'How interesting to meet a real magician ...'
'Do you read palms or entrails?' 'What success
In the alchemic line?' The trumpet sounds.
All pass into the specially built hall
Which cost ten architects and many masons.

Platoons of pallid secretaries surround
Each place, at which are set the texts of long
Insulting speeches. The morning's business starts.
'Before we can permit our boiling oil
To cool we must be sure your catapults
Are pointing from our frontiers.' 'If your spies
Disguise themselves as dervishes, our kites
Will tumble fire-balls on your mausoleums.'

Faust makes himself invisible and gives
The Duke of Seville a buffet on the ear.
This potentate turns to his deadly foe, the Grand
Mufti, and dabs him with his withered arm
And overturns that paralytic Turk,
Whose allies, rushing for the door, collide
With the false friends of Spain. Thrombosis, rupture,
Incontinence of urine, rife in the hall!

Then Faust ignites some Chinese crackers, which
Explode among a group of experts in
Fearsome ballistics. They take flight. And soon
The gorgeous chariots and litters move
Along the dusty roadways of the world.
Faust is alone, and dares the planet's wars
To wound him more than his unease of soul,
Gazing upon the empty towers of man.

The Hittites

Short, big-nosed men with nasty conical caps,
Occasionally leering but mostly glum,
Retroussé shoes and swords at oblong hips –

Or so the stone reliefs depicted them.
But how trustworthy can those pictures be?
Even in that remote millennium

The artist must have seen society
From some idiosyncratic vantage point.
Short, big-nosed, glum, no doubt, but cowardly,

For him, as always, the time was out of joint;
And his great patrons as they passed the stone
Would turn their eyes and mutter that complaint

Whose precise nature never will be known.

Versions of Love

'My love for you has faded' – thus the Bad
Quarto, the earliest text, whose midget page
Derived from the imperfect memories
Of red-nosed, small-part actors
Or the atrocious shorthand of the age.

However, the far superior Folio had
'My love for you was fated' – thus implying
Illicit passion, a tragic final act.
And this was printed from the poet's own
Foul papers, it was reckoned;
Supported by the reading of the Second
Quarto, which had those sombre words exact.

Such evidence was shaken when collation
Showed that the Folio copied slavishly
The literals of that supposedly
Independent Quarto. Thus one had to go
Back to the first text of all.

'My love for you has faded' – quite impossible.
Scholars produced at last the emendation:
'My love for you fast endured.'
Our author's ancient hand that must have been
Ambiguous and intellectual
Foxed the compositors of a certainty.
And so the critical editions gave
Love the sound status that she ought to have
In poetry so revered.

But this conjecture cannot quite destroy
The question of what the poet really wrote
In the glum middle reaches of his life:
Too sage, too bald, too fearful of fiasco
To hope beyond his wife,
Yet aching almost as promptly as a boy.

from *Meredithian Sonnets*

IV

The worker columns ebb across the bridges,
Leaving the centre for the few ablaze.
In bars, fox terriers watch their masters raise
Glass to moustache; and rain streams from the ridges
Of blackened balustrades and capes of girls.
To death and rubbish theatres resound:
Dummies in shops imperfectly expound
The nude: throats raise the temperature of pearls.
Luxury and moderate gaiety disguise
The flight of coin, the absence of ideas.

Doomed certainly, he thinks, and feels the spears
Upon his flesh as he upturns his eyes
Towards the yellow face of time against
The racing sky. So this is the thing it is,
He says aloud, to live in mortal cities –
Haunted by trivial music, stomach tensed.

VI

Mouths pallid mauve, eyes in mock sleepless rings –
However strange the style, the heart responds
To each new generation's browns and blondes
With chaste illegible imaginings.
Girls cluster at the corner of the street
With feathered heads of birds, on legs of birds:
Their high indifferent voices utter words
Whose spell the meaning cannot quite defeat.
Behind, in concrete neutral as a gull,
The slavish windows of the epoch stare,
But through those lips the corresponding air
Emerges with romance ineffable;
And he desires that what he sees will be
Uncovered by a future plough in tense,
Glittering and perfect terms – false evidence
Of fleeting fashion, of his lunacy.

XVI

The wife was in the bedroom: in the attic
The servant slept, her cheek still smeared with ashes
Diaphanous, the bedroom's shifts and sashes:
Around the servant's body, unemphatic
Calico. Yet the evening found his feet
Creaking the attic stair. At first she thought
To hide the hard ebullient flesh he fought
To show, and left him straddling the narrow sheet
The master of her inwardness and tears.

But later nights she was already bare
When he ascended merely to declare
How wild the wind, his loneliness and fears.
Soon he was visiting no more that room,
Preferring to continue to make cower
Beneath its silk the form he lacked the power
To waken, and speak freely of his doom.

Love and Murder

Strange that in 'crimes of passion' what results
Is women folded into trunks like suits,
Or chopped in handy joints to burn or lose,
Or sallowed with poison, puffed with sea,
Or turned into waistless parcels and bestowed
Under the fuel or the kitchen floor.

Perhaps those ardent murderers so prize
The flesh that it disturbs them not at all
To separate an ankle with an axe,
Or contemplate some leathern lady, long
Of the spare bedroom pungent occupant.
Love, after all, must overcome disgust.

We lesser amorists make do with girls
Prim or unfaithful, loud and ageing wives,
Loving too little to implant them deep
Within our guilty dreams where secretly
They would take off their green and purple clothes
To show the unchanging shamelessness of bone.

The Historian

I

The scene my study: Faustian locale!
I speculate on my lack of energy
Before the tempting foolscap, and decide –
My theories staggering, my learning sound –
That I am sickening for a minor ill;
And wonder how in my solitary life,
I caught the bug. Unquestionably I ache.
Two days ago (or was it yesterday?)
I ventured to the city. By the river
The famous towers of our tyrannies
Were half washed out by rain, and I was conscious
Of being part of the infected mass
Hurrying all ways on the ancient bridge.
Even historians catch history.

II

So long sunk in dynastic scholarship,
I look out of the window with surprise
To see bare branches, and the ghostly tits
Ever appear and reappear without
Overt existence in between. The grip
Of winter took my country while the prize
Arcadius to Marcian transmits.
And what the jarred succession was about
Seems, after all, the bearing of the nip
And burning of the planet. That my eyes,
Instead of the world's imperatorial splits,
Now rest upon a rain-debouching spout,
Seems equally irrelevant before
Our curled trajectory from frore to frore.

III

I overlooked your manuscript and saw
(In the quiet room, illuminated by
Culture's immense resources, a candle flame)
'Rescued the world at the brink of the abyss'
And felt a sickly fear. I had not known
That you had also come to this conclusion –
Thinking not of the rescue, the abyss.
I turned away, said nothing, marvelling
At the comparative indifference
Of previous fears. Almost immediately
I realized that *you* meant Diocletian
Or some such name of the unrescued past,
And looked again less guiltily upon
The maelstrom breaking in your youthful nape.

IV

Even more brilliant pupils will possess
Illusions neither reason nor disdain
Eradicate. Astonishing to find
The young full lips, set off by hair and dress
In a bizarre contemporary strain,
Voicing opinions fatuous or blind.
Though even those tender mouths themselves, I guess,
Are put to uses I would think quite vain –
Imprinting merely their own callow kind.
That fear and credulity led to excess
In judging the Vandals' numbers, I explain
Once more. It does not need that to remind
My cultured heart of cracks made by decay
Through which the stunning and uncaring stray.

V

What is he doing underneath the rose tree?
The minnesinger crosses fingers with
A long-haired, gold-haired girl who carries a dog:
He bears a sword, and both are ruddy, smiling.
I realize all at once that this took place
At dawn, and that the afternoon it was
That blasted rose and girl. Were poets gay,
Ready for action, courteously in love?
It seems their ladies thought them knights, their hearers
Of similar material to themselves.
Eventually arrived a century
Of mad old age and horrible mulattos.
The railway sidings waited and the lights,
Visible from here, that stain smoke-scribbled skies.

VI

'Almost invariably a eunuch, the
Grand Chamberlain.' No doubt, no doubt, since he
Would be at times unlikely not to see
Augusta in a bath of milk, or hold
The crapulous forehead of a twelve year old
Curopalates. What undevious, bold
Spirits, the ancients – to create a class
So apt for jobs of consequence, but crass.
How unlike us, whose gelding comes to pass
Not with a stroke but over painful years,
And then – why, then are deemed fit engineers
For the great car of state; or, with our sneers
At vulgar speech and realistic line,
Drive art into a consummate decline.

VII

The dread of barbarization in that late
Empire – impossible to grasp entirely,
Since of the nation that they feared so direly
Many were *princeps* in the cultured state:
Besides, that state itself was ferine. Thus
One cannot help but see this paralleled
In age's censure of the lascivious
To which it is by appetite impelled
In vain – its horror of a licence which
Its earlier tolerance handed to its daughters;
And also in the doctrine that negates
The primacy and nurture of the rich,
Instinctive, sensuous poles of man – from quarters
Where members, doubtless, far from match huge pates.

VIII

They see dark skies of unshed snow behind
The snow-sleeved trees like dancers touching hands.
The northern frontier. Vast unfriendly lands
Far from the groves of red and golden rind
Where, in alfresco schools, the cogent mind
Hatched a philosophy that brought these bands
Of civilizing privates – fate none understands.
To think there is another, strange, mankind!
So nearly indistinguishable from
Barbarians, the inhabitants, that for long
Their masters goggle with inquietude
At women with their hair like pelts, snow-strewed;
Until they are, insidiously as song,
Possessed and haunted by the idiom.

IX

Even the paltry things the unmounted craved
Were wrested from them by the cruel riders.
The tombs of conquerors came to be engraved
With the illegible signatures of spiders.
Dyspepsia and sleeplessness derange,
Instead of opium and octoroons,
The artist's senses. All is senseless change:
History turns to oceans from lagoons,
And from democracy to lethal whims
Of Blues and Greens in violent hippodromes.
And thus the individual life: there brims
A poison of love inside us aged gnomes
That cannot be released; whose citadels
Fall to proliferating barbarous cells.

X

'Names of usurpers in italics' – why
Does putting down this rubric rake my scalp?
For, after all, the catastrophic try
At diarchy (one emperor like an alp
Or jelly) happened to another order.
And when I further muse I feel that these –
That lived along a terrifying border
And wore the clothing of our tragedies –
Though doubtless forked and papped and *sapiens*,
Were not, as we are, man. Hard to conceive
That in the future's culture one will blench
At reading of our state, and not believe
That those who kindled the appalling fires
Were his erect and ordinary sires.

XI

Should the barbarians be not at hand
A dissolute culture will destroy itself.
So it is nothing great that no vile band,
In search of females, stimulants and pelf,
Our frontier happens currently to prowl.
Waking at night, I hear the embouchure
Of locomotive, chimney-pot and owl,
And for our limited and insecure
Kingdom of kindliness and order tremble.
Yes, of that dissoluteness I am part,
But how remarkably can I dissemble
The promethean steadfastness of one whose art
Is doomed to rubble for a thousand years
Before its armless beauty quicken tears.

XII

At least, I tell myself, we do not chuck
Slaves to wild beasts. But still the yearning burns
For springs of culture when the tribe for crowns
Of vegetation raced along the wrack,
And, masked by obvious emotions, played
To sun-lit, wind-swept theatres, in terms
Even more stringent than reality,
That fun or vengeance of the gods, called fate.
Agons not circuses in those far times;
Not sport, gymnastics; not the factory
But lyrics. Though I know my dissident mind
And puny body would have matched as ill
Such innocence and health as these unkind
Years that yield cities to the hawk-nosed will.

XIII

The notion of the Wall and Counter Wall,
For instance, came to them at Syracuse.
The Wall was reared by those who most of all
Were frightened of the unspeakable abuse
Of foreigners transforming Syracuse.
And thus by building this immensely tall
Protection led the investing force to use
The taller cover of a Counter Wall.
I see at every crucial turn of fate
Those soldier-labourers, those citizen-
Victims at their crass, suicidal tricks;
And find, to say the least, inadequate
The rueful groans that rose on all sides when
They turned from love or art to handle bricks.

XIV

You ask me to attend a conference.
The theme: the freedom of the historian.
Venue: a city of ever-changing name.
My hesitation calls to mind our youth,
When we espoused the cause of change, and merely
By adherence hoped to nudge the course of change.
And then I telegraph the message: 'No.'

The journey would involve too much expense.
The congress itself would fall beneath the ban
Of truly free historians. The same
Old points on which I know I have the truth
Will endlessly be brawled. Besides, it's nearly
Time to set out upon a trip more strange
Than ever men as history undergo.

XV

'Zeno was not beloved.' The words promote
At once uneasy stirrings in my soul.
I look up from the text and in a bowl
Of tulips see returned my stringy throat.
Outside, on leafy billows, towers float:
The saint- and beast-carved strongrooms of the whole
Species' achievement. Is my harmless role
Played by permission of the snake and stoat?
Why should I care? The great ones of the realms
Fall soon or late to our recording pens;
Haters of truth, become its stuff at last.
But this is not the dismay that overwhelms:
Youth that brings down or hoists the crown looks past
My work and face with equal indifference.

XVI

Familiar with the Rome of Crassus – that
Famous triumvir and all-powerful
Building-site speculator – I must wonder,
Alive in this metropolis where at
Every street-corner cranes pile cell on cell
To some great lucrative aesthetic blunder,
Why I myself have failed to profit by
The copying in my epoch of the ills
Of history. Impoverished and in lonely
Opposition, even at the stadium I –
Unlike the roaring mass – admire the skills
Impartially. In fact, my hope is only
That blood will not be spilt and that each side
Will with defeat be somehow satisfied.

XVII

The Dead Gate … for an instant the adjective
Seems neutral and innocuous as 'West',
Until I go on to read the thing was used
For carrying corpses out; and I must give
A glance at the passage from my room, so blessed
With awkward corners and by gloom suffused.
I now, in all the lodgings where I live,
Have pondered the arrangements for my rest
Eternal more than the springs on which I snoozed
– Rather as cultures through the purposive
Terror of death left slabs still manifest
In water-forsaken regions; or excused
Questions proposed by iron, water, coals,
By tenderness for the escaping souls.

XVIII

Historical, too, this lady I sometimes visit,
I think, as her bosom props my bearded head;
Her shape determined by the progress in
Mechanical engineering, whaling and
The metal industry. O pink-lit room,
What issues your activities must burke!
I hear the horse of Asia's brutal triumphs
Clop in the little street below, conveying
Suburban theatre-goers. Time to leave.
Goodbye, then, to the mammal attributes
That goddesses had no more of. A moon, so high
One does not see it, silvers stones that seem
Already fit to part and show what had
Originally to be vanquished there.

XIX

They journeyed on and met the careless Queen
And learnt from her to loose the sweat-stained leather.
Their tall propitiatory fires green
With coppered logs, they left in fabulous weather
And sailed above the caverns of the god
Whose dripping daughters hauled their breasts in vain
Above the gunwales. Then the period
At last began. They saw through fertile rain
The shore whose name they'd always known; and landed,
And marked the city out between the hills.
Not one for his posterity demanded
The burning essences that time distils,
With which it brutalizes kings, and dooms
Philosophers to mad and futile glooms.

XX

The myth of Paris and the apple never
Impressed my heart with its significance
Until that part grew elderly. Whichever
Queen got the prize seemed of indifference.
I craved no kingdom; military glory
Absurd for my cowardice; while I was dead
Sure charm could manage that part of the story
Which brought the fairest in the world to bed.
But now I see that Juno and Minerva –
Fine figures of women, doubtless – were in fact
Too womanly for that antique observer
In whom (his being a legendary act)
Apple breasts, thin thighs and fur, uncertain voice
Of girlhood were the more appropriate choice.

XXI

The fleece, the bough, the apple, Persephone,
All things that in the golden age were gold,
We know to have been the images of grain –
The stuff most precious to those men of old,
Which heroes lifted from the dragon's tree,
Which brought the hell-descending husbands pain,
And in pursuit of fleet, breast-trembling girls
Delayed the most eager. Spring revealed the shoot
That summer turned the hue to be desired,
But the same season that they cut the fruit
Held chill disaster. Then the whole race hurls
Itself with weapons on the desolate and mired
Domain. At last reluctantly it yields
The slender queen to sparkling sepia fields.

XXII

It slept: its dreams were powerless to renew
Its former invention, being all of faint
Desires imperfectly recalled on waking.
Its great extremities and capital grew
Withered, incapable of harm. The paint
Peeled from its frescoes and, the gods forsaking,
Column and pediment fell in fields of blue.
And then appeared the mild, self-centred saint
Whose sick environs seemed of his own making,
Who indicated what was good and true
In orders too remote to bear the taint
Of temporal decay. Its heart stopped aching:
Except for crowns the unenlightened hated,
And virgins never to be violated.

XXIII

The Other World's a concept that has seemed
Always far-fetched or puerile to me,
Whether beyond the grave or in what 'gleamed'
Through molecules discrete of alp or sea;
Significance assumed by the unfree,
Appalled by their brief servitude before
Strangler and priest unbolt the prison door.
But see, today I've gazed upon a page
That reproduced a statue's photograph
To show the god of some sand-blotted age.
The head was missing but what held the staff
That ruled the living from the cenotaph
Had fingers each with circumstantial nail.
The long, dark grooves were on another scale.

XXIV

All winter I kept mistaking for a bird
A hanging leaf. And only in old age
Have I admitted it to be absurd
To think Dame Nature not a personage.
So that beyond the window this impassive
Order might hide a pantheon which sighs
For all our woes; or comprehend a massive
Variance in state we can't ourselves surmise
(As though historical process were to end,
Having at last forborne its noblest forces
To corrupt). And imperceptibly will blend
With notions of robot nightingales and horses
Faster than light, the body's ancient skit,
That once seemed destined only for the pit.

XXV

And actually survived. And changed. And made
Them happy with their soil-skinned globe because
The destination of its fruits obeyed
The appetite of reason, weaklings' laws.
Wars ended. No minority of men
Was prejudiced or felt itself to be.
Waking at four, the sensitive had then
Only art, passion or senility
To keep them from the dream-packed rest of slumber.
The planet seemed to spin on such a point
It shocked when summer trembled into umber;
But as the snow enlarged each branch's joint
They lit fires on the river, and befriended
Flocks of strange birds, that fearlessly descended.

3

1963–1977

The Symphonist

To write just too many symphonies
For the memory easily to
Identify; to have made love to
Her in a variety of strange
Rooms and woods; to dream of clear meanings,
And on waking utterly forget …

Is it the Sixth where the initial
Largo is chased by two raspberry-
Blowing rondos? And the Ninth programmed
The withstanding by heroes of the
Siege of the boulevarded city,
Or the gazing at a young harpist.

In some uneasy interlude of
Peace the lake fell. Embedded in its
Strata was her skull, exemplar of
Eye-ridges on their way to thinking.
For 300,000 years or so
The axe-heads scarcely altered their shape.

Then the dream was recalled. It involved
Rolling fire on the far-off plain,
A flight in which she was left behind.
Out of that agony of loss sprang
A score for a thousand voices, and
Seventeen years of complete silence.

Think of quite outrageous conjunctions.
Have the tympani slogged during the
Viola's cadenza. Enfold in
The long hirsute arms two tender breasts
And a white rib-cage unfitted for
A time of ice, of philistine rule.

To make four movements out of four notes;
To end with a transformation of
An early, almost forgotten theme;
To devote a whole life to wordless
Communication … Trumpeters, where
Are your ox-horns? Girls, your rouge for bones?

Chinoiserie

I've always been comfortably off.
In my poorer days my desires were modest:
Now I earn more, my previous habits
Circumscribe the area of my extravagance.
I've tried to take care that being a poet
Didn't get in the way of making a living,
And eventually this other occupation
Actually incremented my income
And stopped hurting my respectability.
It's a toss up whether I turn first
To the literary or the financial page,
And I find it just as painful to read
Of a bonus issue of shares I failed to buy
As of the success of a rival writer.
Yet I can seriously assert
That finally money doesn't matter.
It's supported a life I can't approve of.
I've saved it for a life I shall never enjoy.
Like my neatness and punctuality,
My interest in it denotes a fixation
At the irrelevant anal stage of existence.
If I became penniless tomorrow …
Still impossible to change to a hero of art!
An incurable lack of high seriousness
Is indicated by concern about cash;
A deficiency in the religious sense;
A fatal practicality for life.
Given this species of character,

My follies have arisen from denying it –
Underestimating the greed of others,
And the longevity of capitalism.
How much happier I'd have been
Had I put my patrimony in low-yielders,
And been less timid and considerate,
And voted Tory, and stuck to prose.

Reading The Bostonians *in Algeciras Bay*

For Alan Ross

At the next table, on the terrace
(*The Bostonians* open on my
Knee), a pale pumice domineering
Head; in the prosperous buttonhole
An order. Behind the lush hotel,
Folds of burnt-brown, donkey-littered hills,
Beyond which runs the river with the
Battle-name. Old man, did you, thirty
Years ago, fire shots that killed my friend?

'Whatever money was given her
She gave it away to a negro
Or a refugee. No woman could
Be less invidious, but on the
Whole she preferred these two classes of
The human race.' Though even Henry
Found history grave at last; came to
The 'unspeakable give-away of
The whole fool's paradise of our past.'

On the concrete sheds by the quayside:
PESCADOS S.L., dominating
The life of the town, arsehole of Spain.
In this suburb, round the stinking stream,
An African poverty, from which

The boys emerge, asking for 'money',
Threatening with the mock horns of bulls,
Plucking a pack of Marlboro from
The breast pocket of my ink voile shirt.

Despite the cigarette-evidenced
Yankee subventions, only the jail
And the *plaza de toros* look clean
And in the least substantially built.
And to guarantee the lottery's
Success there are inexhaustible
Supplies of the wall-eyed and crippled
To be led to street-corners by boys
And there reassure the unlucky.

Dear friend, all is still to struggle for.
In our middle age what engrosses
Is the play of human emotions –
In the hotel today, a wedding:
A girl of eleven perturbed at
Her mother wearing only one glove,
Dusting down her elder sister's dress;
Though herself bustless. Illustrative
The guests, of all stages in love's game.

But in that room of our chance meeting
Over the crumby Piccadilly
Of 1944 – did we think
Then to succumb to slide-rule metrics,
Hear social-democratic England
Object to the roasting merely of
Civilians in yet another
Civil war, and to stay *de luxe* in
The realms of a tyrant of our youth?

It's not enough to have chosen
The figurative (and preferably
Front view) to hang on our walls, alas!
Nor to have laughed over luncheon at

Numerous other *littérateurs*,
Borne the medieval and junkie
Blend of today's medical science;
Nor even, in your case, to have slaved
At friendship, and support of the arts.

What a mess, societies of men!
At first spreading out along these coasts,
Leaving their driftwood and turds afloat,
Amphorae capsized by sand, pillars
Broken, democratic orations
Echoing hollowly to lands of
Fog – where, posed as abstract principles,
The punks of a class's lust gather
A patina of factory grime.

As well as with unrequited love,
Dying, and distaste for our own verse,
Shall we always have to put up with
Delusions induced by the very
Apparatus intended to cure –
Sick doctors, nurses with biceps,
And inside the asylum's high walls
Its own individual banner?
Yes, in our time; and in our sons' time.

The Map

A brilliant conjecture indeed,
Where the very shape of our wishes –
Innocence-smooth belly-curve of coast
And single deep safe inlet for our vessel –
Was adumbrated from mere glimpses
Across impossible seas. Peaks rose
From hinterlands of ignorant white,
Twins dimly familiar from childhood;
And even the capricious climate,

The zinc veins, croppable savannahs,
And fern grottos diamonded by torrents
Were indicated on succeeding
Folios. But what are these added
In the margin? Mere fancies of the
Cartographer or croakings of some
Returned, stick-limbed, insane explorer?
Farting winds from gross cheeks of cherubs
Blow trivial devils to the Poles,
Arses revealed by tattered small-clothes.
Supporting the whole, a recumbent
Skeleton, detached fore index joint
Reflectively along a toothy jaw
From which on a scroll the legend winds:
New Found Land, graveyard of fat monsters –
Anchorage ice-locked at all seasons –
Loud gales, crabs in lichen, smell of fish.

Ambiguities of Travel

And will you really wake at the hotel
With the mountain in the garden and the crippled
Gardener? And go to see the wall-paintings
Of the wall-eyed flautists, and the pink sandstone
Water nymph with vulva-exposing embroideries,
And the silk banner (reconstruction) of Lord Kanishka?

Poetry is something between the dream
And its interpretation. Through pleached boughs
Of blossoming, still vivid your pantisocratic
Imaginings, how hurtful to think
Of the past dragging its foot to meet you,
As though a mirror stood at the pathway's end.

A saying of Kanishka: 'Human love —
So much beauty lavished on so much goodness.'
Dear child, it's only that the colours have flaked
That the musicians are so repulsive;
And the sepulchre of the ruler was long ago
Shat on by pillaging baboons.

What song will your mind rehearse as, shaving,
You see the girl still slumbering in the striped light?
That late sonata movement where, trilling each note,
The performer's hands move farther and farther apart?
Strange, both expounding life in likenesses,
Voyaging through the other's boiling wake.

In Memory of My Cat, Domino: 1951–66

Rising at dawn to pee, I thought I saw you
Curved in a chair, with head raised to look at me,
As you did at such hours. But the next moment,
More used to the gloom, there was only a jar
And a face-cloth. Time enough, nonetheless,
For love's responsibilities to return
To me.
         The unique character of the dead
Is the source of our sense of mourning and loss;
So, back in bed, I avoided calling up
What I know is intact in my mind, your life,
Entirely possessed as it was by my care.

I could conceive you not as dead but merely
Gone before me to a world that sends to us
Decreasing intimations of its beings —
No doubt because they find us in the end
Pathetic, worthy, but of small importance.

So long had we been together it never
Occurred to me I might fall somewhat behind.
Even when, familiar fur in my hands,
The sickly wave of barbiturate rose up,
I thought it was I who was journeying on –
But looking back there is only emptiness,
Your dusty medicaments and my portrait
Taken with you: sad mode of life you've outpaced.

Orders

All through the summer a visiting quartet –
Father and daughter blackbird, pigeon, squirrel.
Soft cluckings in the tree announce the blackbirds:
First it was him, daring the dangerous sill;
Later brought his Cordelia of the brood –
She pouting and shivering, rather remote.
Now in her nature like all other daughters
She drives him off the grapes and bread I scatter.
Slate-flat, slate-blue taffeta tail embraced by
Matronly wings, gray marbled evenly gray,
The pigeon drops draughtsmen on the terrace squares,
Patrolling ceaselessly. And in the mornings,
Anxious at the window, one hand clutched at heart,
My chinless friend, with soil-crumbed neurotic nose,
And tail a brush for cleaning babies' bottles –
Disconcertingly like Sam or Sue Squirrel.

This summer, too, I saw in J.B. Bury
'That mysterious prae-Aryan foreworld' –
Not really understanding the phrase, dimly
Conceiving a life before the oil-nurtured
Legions, before the language of short, hard words,
Before the death ships, the bronze, the chalk horses,
Which now survives only as our consciousness
Of the dotty element in our natures,
Or as a tiny, round, thinly black-haired head

Called to the colours from a cretin valley,
Or as the unmemorialled existence
To which we may be doomed.
                        The quite senseless war
Through summer days will run into winter days,
The war that during my life has scarcely stopped.
And the government that I elected, like
All governments, whether elected by me
Or not, will be powerless or uncaring.
How strange that in this sphere my desire should be
Always so different from the general will!

'There is no bridge between directional time
And timeless eternity,' wrote the gloomy
German; 'between the course of history and
The existence of a divine world order.'
Though far from belief in a divinity,
One sees indeed what he meant (and perhaps there
The translator was gravelled for the right word,
As one is oneself) – for certainly what may
Be conceived to be the principles ruling
The stuff that surrounds us, they have not to do
With bird-song, bird-love, the propulsion of metal
Into men. And what but the material
Can ever confront us, its open constants
Expressed on inevitably baffling clocks?

But I am thankful, on the whole, for this chance
To share in irrelevant events – being
In any case borne on to a species of
Significance by the drives of a motive
(No doubt falling far short of the eternal)
That will change my egotistic young blackbird
Next year to a care-worn mother. Take note, you
Gods, how my boyhood began with my father
Reading the news of the killing of young men;
How my adult body struggled with a mind
At odds with the task an unjust world imposed
And broke out in lesions that the mind despised.

Goethe said: 'The idea always appears
As a strange guest in actuality ... The
Idea and common actuality
Must be kept strictly separate.' Very well:
Assign the business of being a poet
To an order of things entirely divine,
And the anguish to its historical material;
And accept the consolation (in Kafka's terms)
Of a wound that precisely fits the arrow.

But suppose the divinities relented,
Said: 'Your existence shall accord with our wills' –
Would our being prove even more frightening?
What would the creatures cry out at our windows,
Dark on a sky of furnace yellows: 'Join us
In the dumbness of utterly pure feeling,
To the forces that stretch you out over time
Surrender, and rejoice in the cellular
Mishaps that must bring about your extinction'?

And what if ourselves became divine, and fell
On the pitiful but attractive human,
Taking the temporary guise of a swan
Or a serpent: could we return to our more
Abstract designs untouched by the temporal;
Would we not afterwards try to get back those
Beautiful offspring, so mortal, so fated?

The Visitors

Powers that seem to arrive from elsewhere, I
Bewilderedly open the door to you, though
I sent out the invitations and, indeed,
Recognize the visages from a lifetime's
    Dreaming of dining with gods.

No one could be more suspicious than I of
The sudden appearance of divinities
In middle-aged verse, but how else to describe
The double nature of nature in epochs
   Of creative happiness?

Besides, little use to recall, strolling at
Dusk on the suburban common with my thoughts
And walking-stick, as I stumble over the
Dung of lions, that in fact in this place a
   Circus encamped some days past.

And the tragedies of our infancy, a
Degree more real than the howl of the guilty
King, we rehearse till our death. No wonder They
Visit us sometimes to remind us of our
   Right to be blessed and consoled.

Well, enigmatic beings, though you lurk in
The gloom of book-shelves and vibrate from the grooves
Of whirling discs, I resolve to devote your
Imparting of blinding connections to those
   Who would spurn the locales.

And assert that your order, somewhat concerned
For our world, demands the expropriation
Of all whose motives are ruled by the fetish
Of things and not by the hominids who at
   Times can enchant even you.

I don't suppose you ever try to enter
The chain-hung doors of terrible rooms where the
Plotting of our downfall goes on. No, it's just
Us you can help, and our enemies frighten
   You more than they do ourselves.

And you never conceived of a species whose
Members could injure each other. In your land
The jealousies and hates cannot matter in
The end because of your immortality.
   That's what you try to confer.

Disasters

Can they be part of our dreams, so disastrous
They wake us, and stay in our life of waking?
Just as the assassin's shell, pitched from a world
Of black suns, and wireless voices in the head,
Comes to lodge in a situation of blood-
   Stained skirts and hopeless sorrow.

Or is it simply not true, the sense we have
Of a life ruined by us, unprompted by
Pre-existing paradigms? Didn't in fact
Primaeval fluids hold terrors for newly
Created proteins about to find out how
   To perpetuate themselves?

And galaxies move in fear of colliding?
But try to conceive the author of a whole
Hierarchy of unease; ineptness, no,
Nor malevolence could account for the lack
Of allegiance of an entire order
   To the rules that expound it.

One sees how legends came to be invented
Of gods, so to speak, picking their noses while
The dolls they'd made tore off each other's fingers,
Or of an atrocious angel whose revolt
Put the divine omnipotence for ever
   At the issue of gunfire.

But such is the rudimentary prattle
Of those whose very birth implanted a sense
Of disgust for their origin. Protest rises
From sunsets cobbled by exploded islands;
Plumage in children's water-colour oblongs;
   From fountain, doorway, rose.

Early in these November mornings, who'll dare,
Passing by portraits of worried-over love,
To open curtains on a world still dark, still
Doubtful of blackbird chinkings, moon-livid still?
The mildly-drugged with coffee and self-regard,
    Language-infatuated!

Symbolist Creator, would we have had you
Leave less to chance and speculation? How else
Except through flight along the margin of the
Permanent, heaving thing could its nature have
So imprinted itself in our sternum pulse
    And arches of our insteps?

Nymphs come from goodness knows what shrines, messages
Between their gravity-neutralizing breasts:
What does it matter, even death and failure,
Utter impossibility of knowing
Their god, so long as a lifetime's aperçus
    Are unsafely recorded?

And the fires lick the violas' bellies,
Algebras lost past recall, great men dateless.
In viable atmospheres breathed on rondures
Far off, the same griefs delicately inflate,
Walking hills like mist, fogging the alleyways
    Of heroic city-states.

Those of Pure Origin

After a throbbing night, the house still dark, pull
Back the curtains, see the cherry standing there –
Grain of the paper under wash of rain-clouds.

No, our disguises are not intended to
Deceive. On the contrary. And could you name
Us we shouldn't be compelled to appear so
Confusingly – smothered in white stars, whistling
Hymn tunes, putting out scaly paws to attract
Attention. Under comic aliases –
Even the specific for insomnia:
Peppermint, lime blossom, betony, scullcap –
We entice you into our dissident realms.
The staggering plots you invent in hours
Abbreviated by anxiety are
Hatched by our logic. Just as when you try to
Talk with the girl of fifteen we tilt her shoe
Inward to imply her different order.

For it's *your* world we're expounding. Don't mistake
Our endeavours. We can't tell you where you're from.
Indeed, despite our immanence we're the last
Who could reveal more than is there already.
Let alone where you're going! Darwin's infant
Enquired about his friend's father: 'Where does
He do his barnacles?' – assumption of a
Universal preoccupation no more

Naive than yours, whether of indifference or
Concern. It's quite plausible that the concept
Of outside disappears outside – in that place
Where nebulae no longer have to awake
And pretend to be happy.

                              Our advice is:
Prefer the less likely explanation.
Different evenings, the evening star appearing
In different corners of the pane – conceive
No senseless revolution in the heavens
But a lucky change of erotic fortune;
A goddess steeped not in urine but in love.
And then so often you've been wrong why shouldn't
You be wrong about the extinction of man?

It's true we tend to avoid you, fatal as
You are in general to our fragility.
But sometimes one of us, whom you knew in flight
And particularly admired for his looks,
Lies down and allows the wind to blow the wrong way
His once glossy pinions. Look into his eye.
It regards you still, though fixed as well on worlds
More real than at that moment you can bear.
Of course, you'll soon take your spade and among
Pebbles, lapis worms, inter the eye from sight.

'Considering my present condition,
I can neither concentrate on poetry
Nor enjoy poetry.' That final letter
May seem a defeat after a lifetime of
Assuming the reality of the art.
Not to us, though it's we are the defeated.
For we boast of our patience – coral *croissants*
Anchored at last to just too-heavy hill-tops;
Laboratories of finches; Galapagos
Of revelation awaiting an observer.
And you, even in the children's puzzle, are
You certain you've seen all the hidden objects?

Yes, there's the extrusion of the wall in
A clawed hump, and a grey frayed rope-end blown round
And round a bough. But what are the abstract shapes
As enigmatic in significance as
Those painters find incised from oceans by arcs
Of a parasol or enclosed from a beach
By the severe bay of a young throat and jaw?

That countenance whose eyes are as pale as if
The flesh had been clipped out to show the ash sky
Behind it … The voice that unavailingly
Says: 'Do you remember taking your laundry
To the woman with elephant legs?'… The past
As ambiguous as hailstones in the gales
Of spring: the future certain – the instant when
You stop being convinced of our existence,
And meaningless that blackbirds masquerade as owls,
That also in the dusk, making free of it
For assignations, jealousies (those affairs
Of energy and waiting unwearying,
Of obsession with menstrual blood), occur
The strange pre-marital flights of humans.

What does it matter that the baptistery proves
As dusty and void as bad nuts when its doors
Provide a progression of style, the basher
Of bronze breaking out from pious platitudes
Into arcades of applied geometry,
Thronged with our perfect but realistic forms?

The mad poet called us, untranslatably:
'Those of pure origin' – left you to divine
Whether we rise from phenomena or,
Perhaps more likely, also require your presence,
As the cathedral the plague, pity the war.

But how can we pretend our hemisphere-wide
Lament, the random trickling and joining of tears
On acres of glass, is entirely for your

Predicament – as your lives, borne upon the
More and more dubiously physical, move
To regions of abnegation and concern
Whose angels we are; though, under cruel casques,
Our curls, our thick, parted lips ever youthful,
Complexions marked with still unmalignant moles
Of the actual, scabs on unfolding leaves?

Afternoons

Mothers with taller daughters, shopping
In afternoons, what sustains your lives?
Here's a pair of crimson plastic lips
Left over from a Christmas cracker:
To which generation shall I offer it?

Conceived after the last of wars that surely
Could possibly lead to works of art.
Shall these saplings be hacked down?

Like bluebells in a wood the uniforms
Through the palace railings. Some insane inscription
Cut from a poet's elegy
Identifies the ill-horsed author of carnage.

De-birding jelly, black with grime, on the shaven
Polls of the persians – a savage concept of coiffure –
Has failed to shift the sense of a plaza
Snowing with fragments of brain, the pavement stained,
Debris of an exploded urban dream.

Towers strike out the time for tea,
The time of rehearsals, the time before
The hard liquor of old age. Come in
From your gazing at stockings long as prunus boughs
For almost calfless legs,
And open patterns for knitted bed-jackets

To the jangling of guitars. Poor Gorgons –
Doomed to decapitation in the very
Instant of parturition; the question is
How to prolong your breeding
Of the Muses' continually defeated favourites.

Windows

Easy to tell how habitually I
Look through these great spectacles that enlarge the
Soul's eye – so that sunsets, for instance, of quite
Undifferentiated madder seem to
Possess the glamour of unapproachable
Geniuses, in an existence apart.

Sometimes the sky has a ghostly lampshade or
Countenance watermarked in it, as if it
Were making abundantly plain its divorce
From phenomena; for although the lenses
Intensify perception, to the object
Their attitude is deeply ambiguous.

Should a bird come out of the darkly-banked trees and
Alight on a seat's conveniently bent
Arm, one sees that its pupil (if a pigeon)
Is not, as one thought, the core of a target
But oblate, as though to keep tripping, while it
Revolves, some shaft from a dangerous image.

And one's fingers against the pane are stopped, by
A force that whitens the nails, from seizing the
Dove in their grasp. How tender the world outside
Seems to be, how full of things one could adore –
Were it removed, then, this manner of vision,
Should I fall in the wings of a vast embrace?

Or rather a climate of lunar harshness
Wither my hopes? These tears on the glass are shed
From beings outside with sorrows so huge as
To overwhelm our pity; and not even
Our miniature fires are really printed
On the darkness that incessantly comes down.

Departures

No, I'll not let you go yet, sweetest
Girl, though you ache to depart from my
Boring house, where you're fed with the crumbs
Of experience, loved with the most
    Perfunctory of kisses.

I've something still to tell, if only,
As to a comfortable old wife,
The trivial news of the day, how
I avoided drowning an insect
    In the lavatory at dawn –

Where cyclamen leaves on the lighter
Tone of the window brought to mind the
Lotus in those banal surroundings
That the hour made mysterious;
    Prince Buddha in the passage.

Or perhaps you'll reveal to me why,
Say, the well-concealed Schoenbergian
Mathematics of art have meaning
In the actual intervals, and
    Tremblings of the finger-pads.

As you make a tough, Guinness-drinking
Quintet aware of an odd man out:
That flautist, is he the emperor
Or even perhaps the composer,
    Playing too many wrong notes?

Unworthy to receive your embrace,
I'm always resolving to do much
Better in future, an eternal
Unsatisfactory boy; somehow
　Believing that I will, too.

Possibly I'll dare to write my last
Songs for soprano. Certainly, you –
Exciting and wholly unexplored
Landscape of secret features – sometimes
　Hold out encouragement.

And even when all else fails, the child
That emerged from my truest because
Uncritically accepting life
Will blessedly know of your demands
　And help warrant the future.

For you can't pass in the street, as though
You didn't know them, quite all my race.
Dear Muse, as I grow older you get
More desirable, and in your youth
　(Theoretically free)

You tantalize with the innocence
Of the unpossessed; even the cross
Between your slight breasts seems to render
The transcendental a prey of the
　Conceivably possible.

Besides, since you represent the whole
Human world, your being continues
Apart from the favours you fail to
Bestow, and it matters not at all
　That your slave weeps in his room.

Yes, it's only the deprived who can
Appreciate the beautiful life
Of the entirely committed to
Providing an area in which
    Wrong proteins can make marvels.

Future readers, whose predecessors
Expectedly neglect me, may find
I spoke truly of our posthumous
Life they are enjoying, because of
    My dull faithfulness to you.

What cosy times we've had together,
Playing the gramophone, sipping scotch
And soda; and I very often
Not even getting as far as the
    Nylon cords behind your knee.

Apples are clinging to yellow boughs,
Fruit that the birds have made
Decayed moons; in the false cover of
Fallen leaves, pink worms: drapes just meeting
    Across the stage of corpses.

We look to you to bring to cities'
Repetitive machinery skies
Of marine splendour behind marble
Porticos where Baudelairean
    Hand-maids are already nude.

But should it be thus that the body,
Otiosely ill and naturally
Deficient, appeals to a goddess
It knows to be a figment of its
    Death or of its thoughts of death?

No, the best should await with humble
And excited awe your routine calls,
And dogged life itself must tempt you
To descend, or whirl to remotest
    Quasars in flurries of apes.

Last Sheet

… Suddenly it's autumn, I think, as I look in the garden –
A gloomy dripping world, tree-tops lost in cloud.
Is it possible that anyone so silly can
Write anything good? I don't hear, like poor Virginia,
The birds outside the window talking Greek. I see
My blackbird visitor and wonder where he sleeps,
As sleep he must. And catch my face in the pane,
Becoming ancestral, a cartoon of the mask
To which I've always been indulgent. And turn
To put a disc of Debussy on the machine:
This is what I'd have written had I had genius.
A pity to have got so far along the road
And then never arrived. Give my regards to the Minister
And tell him I've drafted a comprehensive instrument
For the administration of suburbia.

This is the time the robin starts to sing at dusk,
Like a cog catching on cardboard, but the human throat
Is not subject to seasons except those of the withering heart.
They're trying to cure me of my maladjusted glands –
Amusing; rather like trying to change the art of Sickert:
'I've always been a literary painter,
Thank goodness, like all decent painters,' he said.
One can joke, but nevertheless the situation is tragic –
A human lifetime's limited store of eggs, and then
Their very last descent into the longing womb.
It's certainly on the cards that I shall never write
Another letter. This will have to stand, as usual,
For the prodigies I was about to tell you of,
For the connections I never quite saw, the melodies
Played gently while the beauteous statue reconciled
The jarred generations, and Sicily and Bohemia.

Deficiencies

They will look up: 'You never really saw
Those objects we placed on earth for men to name.
Even the trivial hours need not have harmed you
Had you acknowledged the divinity
Of all that wasted your life.' No use to claim
How well I visualized the stinking gloom
Of the wharf where just then I'd docked, the stink being me.

Tiny Tears

Life is an epiphenomenon of the hydrosphere

J.D. Bernal

Strangest fossil in a place of fossils –
The navel of the barely nubile girl,
Disturbing the disturbing slenderness,
Making the illusive fragility
Plausible, the *pâtisseur*'s final flourish.

Open the great library of the cliffs:
Pressed between stiff blank leaves an ammonite's
Very occasional coiled impression,
Pathetic souvenir of a fatal
Visit, to a world, to the mothering sphere –

Which eternally receives coolly her
Offspring, who to live have enclosed her wet
Saltness in membranes of varied splendour
And complication, truly analogous
To polythene, as one might have expected –

The very material of the doll
Called Tiny Tears, whose ambiguity
Of urination resides less in her
Crude thigh sockets than in her creator's
Modesty. Even her weeping throws doubt

On our sorrow for slightness lost or
Never possessed. Quite otherwise the case
Of the distinguished, unpossessable,
Utterly nude, competitive beauty,
Who sails in streaming from archetypal parts.

How can be questioned the emotions of
The procreant goddess? She at least must
Truly love. Our models, so plausible
In essential apparatus, are doomed
To be dismembered by the shores of their birth.

When the tide goes out, small heads, wristed hands,
Are left in the wrack among the litter
Of tougher experiments – comic-book
Monsters' green hair; pointless ribbons; flora
From prehistory. Somehow reassuring.

The Unremarkable Year

The great thrushes have not appeared this year,
No more the sickness of excessive
Evacuation. Taking one year
With another the debits and credits seem to cancel out.

When I recall the family
That fell like a camouflaged platoon
On the garden in 'sixty-eight
(Or was it 'sixty-nine?) I can't help feeling regret.

But there is much to be said for a summer
Without alarms. The plum crop is modest,
The monarch has remained unchanged,
Small differences only in one's teeth and hair and verse-forms.

There'll be no memories like the visit
Of the orchestra of *gamelangs* –
Enhanced by the naked mamelons
Of the dancers – influence that goes on reverberating.

So that the year of painting the shed,
Of missing strange calls, deep dappled breasts,
Is also that of harmonies
That have made one's life and art for evermore off-key.

Georgic

I

It trickles in my palm like blood, the plum juice,
And on this premonitorily autumnal morning –
Small pebbled windfalls, pyrocanthus berries
Clustered and flushed as from tropical marines –
It comes to me that I'm drinking the elements,
Even the snow-flakes, filtered through and syphoned up
         Out of my freehold wedge.

Retire to your estate, the world commanded,
As though sick of a writer they'd never even read.
Well, what now will emerge can scarcely be
Considered more gripping, a smallholder's journal, spiced
With jottings of a temperate climate's changes.
Back in my study, how can I help but envy
         The tragic, the large editions?

No use to comfort my ordinariness to say:
All's a projection from domesticity –
The incest of the gods, the islands of
Revenge. And even monarchs, did they really
Contrive to elevate their actual murders
And greed to planes above the sordid? No,
         But poets sustained the illusion.

A warning to myself about this book:
Don't sabre the leaves too far ahead – though fear
Or constant anticipation of extinction
Is certainly no decent surrogate
For the sense of ampler life one's deficient in.
A note to take cuttings of hardy shrubs is mingled
            Fatally with apophthegms.

II

Sometimes the young die young, as birds in summer:
A corpse against green, incongruously plump.
A day of trivial labours passed, I think
In the September evening how prolonged
The wait to hear a thrush's evening song.
The losses of a year can't be repaired,
            Even granted another year.

The sun behind a tree, straight lines of light
Arrange themselves around a half-masked face;
Obliging science, each tends towards the centre.
Photography might crudely get the point:
But where are the painters whose technique, their whole
Ambition, will make the marvellous plausible,
            Enamoured of appearance?

Equally, what words of mine will show that faces
Of horses and men are unchanged through history?
I mean that among the hillside vineyards or
Overcheck hedgerows, in hoods or under caps,
Rope-haltered or caparisoned in scalloped
Scarlet, still wend the terrible masters
            Of a well-meaning earth.

The Card Table

Today it spends its life against a wall:
Facilities inside quite unemployed.
Its top can be unfolded and a leg

Swung round to make a battlefield of baize
With shallow cups to hold one's cash or chips
And zinc-based corner circlets for the drinks.

It comes down from my father and my youth.
Round it sat Issy Gotcliffe and the Weinbergs,
Powers in the textile trade in Manchester.

There I first stole an aromatic sip
Of scotch, midst laughs at my precocity:
Could be the last year of the First World War.

World vanished, almost in the mind as well –
Too young, my brother, to remember it.
All, save we supernumeraries, dead.

What point or virtue in remembering it?
Except to make it stand for everyone's
Possession of such a world – and of their loss.

The bearded faces carved upon the table's
Thighs (so to speak) will quite soon start to mean
Part of his childhood to another child.

His father will have had the enterprise
To lay out cash for art – extravagance
Condoned by delight and use, as ought to be.

My album of those days reveals that Issy
Served in the infantry – maybe in fact
He perished there, for all is speculative

In my recall, I'm sure; as history is.
At any rate, perhaps he never knew
How fascists tried to exterminate his kind.

Even in '18 he of course looked back
To times astoundingly myself had glimpsed –
A general peace, long days, illusive art.

'*Komm in den kleinen Pavillon,*' they sang –
Of *décor* amateurs would now reject:
Their heroes walrused; stout *grisettes*; and gay

Ill-fitting uniforms, to be exchanged
In a few years for real ones of field-grey.
Ah, music, not made cynical by Weill;

Love innocent in art and so in life;
Empires not cruel save through carelessness;
Summers of mere manoeuvres, courts of cards!

Shakespeare and Co

'Tis strange that death should sing

King John

Late Beethoven quartets: Stravinsky, old,
Murmuring 'Wonderful! Incredible!'
– Which leads the memoirist to name a third

'Who might have joined them', he who 'out of some
Terrible suffering' wrote *Macbeth* and *Lear*,
Then in his final years emerged to give

'Supreme expression' of the sense of life,
To wit *The Tempest* and *The Winter's Tale*.
One's touched, in the context, by this corny view,

Though sure that suffering's what we all can share
With genius and it needn't be top-notch.
The Victorian painter, Richard Dadd, who stabbed,

He said, 'an individual who called
Himself my father', made for forty years
In Broadmoor wonderful, incredible fairy worlds.

The difference is the hand's resource and craft
That turn the cloudy visions of the mind
Into a change of key, a pacifist isle.

Still, strange enough that autumn period:
The fruit so easily could be detached
But nature through its thread hangs on to add

Colour to seeds, a variegated cheek,
Flesh ready for consuming. Chaos persists –
The troublesome reign, false friends' conspiracies –

Though far from the ailments and obituaries
That almost daily plague old age, but yet
Can't spoil (that, rather, must enhance) the sense

Only possessed by age – that, when all's said
And done, life isn't death, however frail
The finger following the heavenly score.

Elephants, Ants, Doves

801 – an elephant in Gaul!
They speak about the stagnant Middle Ages,
Of Islam cutting off the Middle Sea,

And yet the monster enterprisingly
Shuffled from Indian jungle to the Rhône.
Puzzling to tell one's place in history.

What lies before us now – a 'dark age' or
An all too necessary rebirth? A worse
Election looms because of man's new power

To liquidate not merely heretics
And enemies of state but life itself:
Life only geared to nature's cataclysms –

These ants that put their winged friends on their feet,
Like aircraft handlers, and those pigeons which,
From mutual nibbling at the exiguous face

And thrusting a bill far down the other's throat,
Take their respective postures in a sketchy
Rehearsal for prolonging pigeon life.

Social and private failure and success –
How like the human! But without its guilt
And its articulate recrimination.

Yes, I would sacrifice mankind if that
Could save the six-legged and the avian.
Though who's to say the formic city less

Unjust than ours, and that the dove, evolved,
Wouldn't impose tyrannical modes of love?
Let's pension off the soldiers, see what comes.

The Voyage

Suppose yourself alone upon a ship;
The ocean bare, the vessel under way.
Suppose a hand emerges from the deep

To grasp yours and you take it, not afraid,
But kneeling on the hard deck, welcoming
Its pull to an element inimical …

Essential Memory

Fourth of October 1973:
I pick the date to form a line of these
Iambics that keep falling in in threes.

Future historians, and epistolists
On cyclic weather patterns to *The Times*,
May note that I still wore a summer suit.

The bloody oblong that the creeper seems
Beyond the lavatory's striated pane
Astonishes the calls of nature still.

Its life, however, must be told in days.
And even Auden, unforgettable
Because of his creativeness, begins

To fade as what he was: the body – loved,
Or awesome but indifferent natural object –
Breaks up beneath the top-soil of Kirchstetten.

The tractor crawls along – is making! – that
Curved difference between the green and brown
Upon the tilted upland. Here is what

Essential memory depends upon.
For if the plough should fail, the superstructure
Collapses. Howard Newby tells me that

The night of Auden's death he was himself
In Vienna, near that fatal-roomed hotel,
Not knowing Auden there, still less his end.

As what he was. In spite of Howard's health,
Comparative youth, quite soon none will recall
What Auden's 'world' was like when first created.

Autumn: the leaf more insecurely hangs
Than hung the fruit. Nights longer. Weather worse.
Noise of the rain brings other noises near.

Can we love retrospectively the dead
We never really knew? I start to think so;
Especially since there is no question of

Unwished for or unrequited love. And now
The blood's all trickled to the ground; the voice
Only on tape; speculatively warm the clasp.

Late November

Even at two light's slow decline begins:
Hardly worth starting more affairs of day.
Let's doze, then drink some tea and watch the clouds …

Moon in the west sky, ready to be gilt:
Just time before the scotch and poetry
To go and get my shoes – soled, quarter-heeled.

A lady with a pug-dog on a lead
Is saying at the counter how he's been
Attacked by un-led dogs upon his way.

I ask her why I haven't seen of late
The dog at large in our secluded lane.
Reply: 'I never let him off the lead.'

It turns out there's a *doppelgänger* pug.
Do all pugs look alike? It may be so.
Perhaps the freely wandering pug is dead.

Yes, the route home's illumined by the bright
Sliver of moon. The frosty air compels
Breathing as noisy as the squash-nosed pug's.

The curtains drawn, loudspeakers speaking Kern,
I start to wonder what should body out
Astounding images and silvery words –

Canine personae, moon-glow, comic life?

Strange Meeting

In Boots the Chemists an oldish fellow bars my way –
An eye to eye encounter as I try to pass
Into another part of the emporium.

He wears a sober navy overcoat. His hair's
Indubitably salt and pepper. His regard
Is one of semi-recognition, tinged with alarm.

As may already have been guessed, I've misconceived
A mirrored wall as a communicating door.
I turn with a muttered oath: the old boy disappears.

The young boy still continues on his foolish course.

From the Joke Shop

'Why doesn't somebody buy me false ears?'
I can't help remarking as I pack the same,
Plus a few boils and scars, in Christmas paper.

Returning from a stroll some hours later,
I see my ears are big and red enough.
Even a scar may be discerned. Life-long

Ambition to amuse fulfilled, it seems,
Without adventitious aid. Although some boils,
God-given, might more surely make for laughs.

The Future

It's early February. Snowdrops crowd
As close and with as coy dropped heads as some
Green-leotarded, white-capped *corps de ballet*.

Dusk; and a robin sings in actual moonlight.
Ambiguous time; my birthday time. One year,
A frozen waste; another, song and dance.

Rhubarb's sore fingers peep already after
'The mildest January since '32' –
Year of my twentieth; month, no doubt (I don't

Recall!), of bonus kisses out of doors.
What wretched verse I surely then produced
(All luckily destroyed or in a trunk).

But then I apply the epithet to that
Produced in '42, *et cetera*.
I come indoors and play my latest discs.

There seems to be a basic mode of art
To aim for in this troubled epoch yet,
As well as did the eight-years-old Mozart:

Below a melody *cantabile*,
A busy figuration; what the sleeve-
Note calls the *singenden Allegro-stil*.

However, useless envying those who wrote
In more auspicious periods for taste –
No part of artistry is automatic;

Artists' self-betterment the least of all.
This other sleeve-note's wet but right: Poulenc
'Listened to the little song he had within.'

A third pronounces that 'The *guzlas* dream
As they accompany the serenades' –
Phrase from an unknown Wallace Stevens poem!

Better than I, birds sense the future's here
And even in the sudden creamy snow,
Cow-clapped next morning from a false-ceilinged sky

(Making the ballet's *décor* Muscovite),
Still swear to take the decades on and on.
Somehow they hear the *guzlas* dream: as ever,

Their love *alfresco* and their singing spry.

Being

The dead of night. Strange sound. Unknown
Its origin. Perhaps it's in my head –
Some tumour starting to batten on my brain,

The hissing inviolate and continuous.
The February moon is full and almost
Bright enough, it seems, for me to tell

The colours so far showing round the lawn:
The six-rayed open yellow crocus suns;
Quite blue emerging leaves of daffodils.

The latter's gold I'll hope also to see,
Noise from the growth inside my cranium
Being assigned now to a fizzing gram

(See-sawing in my bedside tumbler) of
Ascorbic acid, prophylactic for
The winter's microbes (soon to disappear).

Pauling's authority in science made
Respectable this surely occult faith,
And so converted me a second time!

The hypochondriac will war against
The common cold but has to leave his guard
Wide open to the wrongly-turning cell.

Non-being wasn't in the least unpleasant:
Why should we worry at returning there?
Clearly because of this magnesium moon;

Flowers lancing through what's sepia and rotten;
Affection and respect. O months just past
Of lenient nature, ruthless human loss!

Our years arrive and go, not all forgotten.

Two Muses

Just as I thought that death could never end
Evenings of aqua vitae, writing verse,
So I ignored the Spartan lust to lead
The League – and found myself in Spartan jails.

Or, rather, only too keenly felt the threat
Of that displeasing ideology!
It haunted my quiet felicity as much
As expectation of a drawn-out death.

Sunsets were never smug: witness my odes.
The life not uniformly contemplative:
See, in my souvenirs, the years when I
Was quartermaster to the Seventh Horse.

And yet the element of self-delusion
Asserted itself so often one might think
It was in human nature to be calm;
To be united, human destiny.

Who could have summoned up his naked child
Running along some road, her back on fire?
He would have surely told himself: 'Before
That stage the rules of folly will have changed.'

A memory rises of the former war:
One of our stallions, upper lip retracted,
Its somewhat rubbery implement unsheathed,
Alarmingly trumpeting with so-called love.

Awed by the frenzied drive yet pitying
The creature in its toils, I wondered if
The joined and slanting teeth were pincering
The filly's neck in rage or tenderness.

And wondered whether to be safe from force
Would have to be installed a matriarchy.
Now in my less erotic years I see
Fathers are selfless, too. And mothers … well.

Touching that jailors sometimes still appear
To belong to the human species: though who can tell
The significance of that? Conviction veers
Between condemning Nature and the State.

Thrusting tin plates of beans before your nose,
They say: 'We sang your songs on windy plains.'
Doubtful. They say that slumber is forbidden –
Rather more like the men of will they are.

That women can be aggressive, too, is known
By comics and benedicts. Children grow to hate
Or ridicule the customs of the nest,
Even the clever artifact itself.

Still, they must improvise their own in time.
Still, we've no hope but that of creature love –
Which the deformed give most, the very ones
Sparta leaves out to perish on its hills.

They said: 'You're an early number in our book.
We took you over from your own lot's list.'
Precisely: were they wise, states and their brass
Need only murder us and not each other.

Artists imagine that they serve the nation –
Mostly against its will. My case: preventing
A few from being shot. The relevant
Passages weren't made much of by my class.

It little matters I remain obscure;
I've had so much from poetry and life.
Can't even care about posterity's
Possible benison. Dear jailors, go

Off duty to live those lives you think secure;
Torture your children mildly and your wives
And get what comfort comes from leisure time
And being for a little while top dogs.

The plate, once symbol of advancing culture –
Ore that drew travellers to dusty lands:
I dream of making arms of it again,
As though its limpness might defeat the bronze.

As though such counter-violence, being weak,
Could be excused. As though the chanting Muse
Were forced to bear the obnoxious duties of
Her suffering eldest sister, History.

Ghost Voice

I

We're in the second phase
Of my truancy. At first
Your grief seemed merely designed
To prove my virtue: for me
The greatest sacrifice
Giving up the everyday.
But now I almost enjoy
This liberty bizarre:
Responsibilities gone
I'd forgotten were tyrannies;
Even no need to fret
About your diurnal tears.
And I see you too have changed
Your habits: freedom has come
To draw on my estate,
To let out a social sob,
To sketch another life –
Effaced, the desire at my death
To be absent for ever yourself.

II

Like you, we absentees with certainty
Can't meet the lost ones of our former lives.
And yet we see more clearly that they form,
With us, a whole confederacy of truth.
For in our novel state they'll never be
Forgotten, as they are in your sad world –
Often by dwindling agents of remembrance.
Scarcely-named siblings, dead in babyhood,
Are here recalled, with visionary force
Now the design's last curlicue is traced.
And, our disguises left behind (spies' hats,

Executive flannel and retired man's slacks,
Each offering a problem of disposal),
Play-acting is no longer possible.
But we suppose you well aware of that
Since our rhetorical gestures of farewell –
Odes, epitaphs, that moved you, though drawn up
By the still-alive – have now been really made.

III

I seem to hear you say
'Don't make too strenuous
An effort to return.'
Are you afraid to have
To live with terminal
Disease a second time
Or that you envisage
The graveyard's further ravage
Of the slight thickness on
The bone, that held your love?

Or has your loss already
Changed to a kind of art
Where the obtrusion of
A hasty scribbled note
(Its source) would give away
The immortality
Your life's emotions claim?

To your notion, whatever the cause,
Belongs an essential truth:
Humankind's recognition
Of time outside human scale –
Even the deathbed blaze
Of once beneficent suns.

IV

Why do we return? Not in the darkened rooms
Of rattling tambourines and butter muslin;
But as you boil an egg or make the bed
    You hear us and answer: 'Darling?'

Yes, that's our wish, after all, whatever ancient
Boredom or intervening cause of unwelcome
Would face us, for our presence once again
    To be taken all for granted.

We don't come in actuality, alas!
For we're in a place that even cosmologists,
Speculating on collapsed stars and anti-matter,
    Couldn't find more alien.

Hedge-Sparrows and House-Sparrows

Our medieval fathers simply named
All small birds sparrows. Hence the absurdity
Of calling these March strangers to the garden
Hedge-sparrows. Bills not the pyramids required
For seed-cracking, chassis altogether longer,
More Italianate, and striped along the back,
This couple trill as constantly as late
Beethoven, restless in trees, and skimming to the border.

I read, you nest in April. Stay till then
And populate our homely area
With dashing aviators, tireless songsters.
But how will you survive the silent hedge-cats
Consoling, too, mankind's suburban life;
Find nourishment, in face of chemical
Warfare against our little green invaders?
I hope my welcome's not as treacherous as Cawdor's.

No wonder that the name's a term of endearment –
'Let me but kiss your eyes, my sweet, my sparrow.'
Even the man-sized ostrich some will know
As the sparrow-camel. Sparrowcide denotes
Destruction of sparrows. Preserve us from that crime.
Instead, let there be sparrowdom, the reign
Of sparrows, for sustaining your kin in name
At least suggests some worth in human habitations.

1935–75

The toothless men of Sind; a faceless lamb;
Hairless mutations of the Norway rat;
The Ishmaels and the Roosevelts; the big
Robertson strain of the Washington navel orange;
Three kinds of triplets; silver guinea-pigs;
The giant salivary chromosomes;
A year of sterilization in Germany;
And polydactyly in swine, in humans –
Having conveyed it home, I wonder how
I could initially have baulked (through sheer
Meanness) at buying from the outside stall
The gathered issues of *The Journal of
Heredity* for 1935.

The Old Toy

Bits of me keep falling off;
bits don't work properly;
and other bits are broken
by the girl who owns me.

O vanishing teeth that crunch
things I still love; O part
I know can't now be mended;
O miniature heart!

from *In His Sixty-Fifth Year*

1976 Draws to a Close

Youth happens only once. I mean, my dreams
Were of us kissing; but being sixty-four –
The age I really am – she as she was
When first we met and fell in love – the world,
I knew, would be censorious to see
A young girl wasted in an old man's arms.

They seek a mate for George and if in vain
He well may be the last one of his kind –
Sub-species of the weird Galapagos
Tortoise, already sixty years of age.
(Though reading on I'm reassured to find
He's likely to clock up a hundred more).

In the same issue of *The Times* I see
That dead at eighty-five, in Munich, on
Tuesday, November thirtieth, is Rasp –
Sinister villain of the cinema
Of Lang. I guess it was 1931
In a flea-pit that still clung to silent films,

On the back row, I watched *Die Frau im Mond*
And through her hair Fritz Rasp, abrasive as
His name. The passion of specific years –
Never repeated – unrepeatable …
Yet strangely I class myself with George, as did
No doubt old Rasp, in Germany, last week.

Singing, 1977

For most of my life, no need to wear specs.
Now I look over them at meetings
With the aplomb of a rotten actor,
Push them around my bumf when spouting,
Needlessly checking the earpieces' hinges.
Of all my portraits I say: poor likeness.
'Colonel (Retired)' or 'Disgusted' stares out,
Doomed to expire of apoplexy;
Whitening moustache, jaw-line sagging.
Like a woman, I think: I've lost my looks.
Reactionary views, advanced mostly
To raise a laugh – taken as gospel!

I've bought these discs of piano music
By Granados – largely unexplored;
And if asked who I'd take to a desert island,
Him or who'd be just as novel, Schoenberg,
Who doubts an elderly buffer would choose
The melodious Debussyan Spaniard?

As a matter of fact I'd not mind taking
The words and music of Johnny Mercer,
Even discounting what really biffs me –
That after the euphemistic 'long illness'
He died in a year of his seventh decade
(Strange years, and each year seeming more strange),
The departed gold summer of '76.
Only the weather will return in the vintage,
Perhaps a corked bottle or two recalling
How bitter some days were to swallow,
Prompting thanks for more commonplace years.

Mercer's pushing the case, of course;
As we do in Cheltenham or Tunbridge Wells.
My life's been a story of ignorance.
I never even used to know
How spiders adhered to walls in winter

(Like blots that need blowing up to be decoded),
Challenging man to accept hibernation;
That wind keeps old folk, like babies, wakeful.
No record made: passion undeclared.

At the junketings for my son's sixty-fifth
I'll be pinching his thunder by nearing
My ninetieth. Not that he'll mind.
Jerome Kern's 'They'll never believe me'
(Pre-dating the torpedoing of Granados!)
And that mysterious Mercer line,
As though from an Edwardian operetta:
'There's a dance pavilion in the rain' –
Things I so often sing, by then
Mad time will have made even quainter.

But could I possibly still own a voice?
Curious enough at sixty-five –
A blessing, too; that sons may note at forty –
Even though one messes about perversely,
Trying, say, four-beat unrhymed lines
Which no decent poet, except Arthur Waley,
Has ever managed to get off the ground.

And why so ego-centred the content?
Emblematic, I try to persuade myself,
Of the entire human condition –
Composers who die in usual pain,
Who drown, meaning to rescue their wives,
Regular soldiers, rain-moulded dancers,
Work of joy and disappointment,
Life of creativeness and bereavement …
Peering at some enigmatic blot,
Groping for my glasses in the night-time.

from *Quatrains of an Elderly Man*

In the Night

I wake up, vaguely terrified, at three
And switch the light on, reach out for my book,
And slip inside the life of sanity
Of Wopsle, Gargery and Pumblechook.

Poetry and Whist

How enviable Herrick's
Fourteen hundred lyrics!
– Though, as the Scot complained when they dealt him all
The trumps, a lot of them were small.

Ordinary Seaman

The 143ft mast of HMS Ganges *at Shotley, Suffolk, has been listed
as a monument by the Department of the Environment*
News item, 1976

Inscribe thereon that in 1941
I climbed it twice in fright.
Once as routine but also (to make sure
I dared) the previous night.

Winter

I step from the house at nightfall, thereby knowing
How startlingly life continues in the wild –
Far traffic's pedal, trees very quietly growing,
The air as cool as kisses of a child.

4

———

1977–1989

Years

Islands of girls, ianthine seas
Even in their eyes –
How long ago he sailed from these!

Plucking a crumpled leaf,
He watches a great moon of winter slip
Its cypress cloud.

Night-sensitive sight and finger-tip
Convey a sense of grief
That mimics natures grief –

Meaning that arguably insane
Cellular order and disarray
Of sepia girls and ageing men.

This summer, earwig season,
Followed the year of ladybirds.
Now, like the cycles of Cathay,

The years inherit labelling words
From which time steals the reason –
Forgetting how, day after day,

The paleface squaw was burnt as brown
As the half-pips that choppered down,
Turning dry grass to flowerets;

And how in the next year's cool
The differently tender fool
Drew from a bucket in July

A shapeless struggling that
On the same trembling finger-tip
Changed slowly to a fly.

Autumn 1981

I nearly say: This is a happy time.
– You far from well; myself
With quite a shopping-list of fleshly ills,
And on the verge of seventy, you
Not far behind.

Our diary: dates with the dentist – putting off
Friends who'd put up with us;
Nor seeing even dearer ones enough.
Recluses who have very nearly
Ceased to mind

The world. Could be a mustering of milk
Bottles announces our end –
The sort of commonplace I often make
A jest of, though suspecting your
Grin's merely kind.

And always I refrain from mentioning
Happiness, unsure
Whether at bottom you don't feel a lack;
And also fearful that the word
Itself unbind

Some spell; and worse befall. Hell fire, worse will
Befall! Meantime, verse, discs,
Et cetera, owned, idly listened to, for years,
Suddenly yield their melodies:
Or so I find.

Earlier, undoubtedly I fiercely loved:
Why else would I have lavished
My miser's store, hung on through jealousy?
Yet now appears the most delicate bloom,
On the death-poised rind.

On the 160th Anniversary of the Discovery of the First Quarto of Hamlet

I'm thinking of throwing away my dressing-gown –
The 'summer' dressing-gown, of thinnest wool.
Dark green and black and terracotta stripes,
The colours of some Victorian cricket club;
Repaired by me dim years ago when far
Beyond repair. An alternative would be
To give it to 'wardrobe' at the BBC,
Their slightly period rails. No art could fake
Its thorough tatters at the arse and pap,
Its *exposé* of lining at the cuff,
Its girdle frayed almost as a squirrel's tail.
Though what role would it help an actor chap
To act? Where in contemporary repertoire
Resides a miser formerly quite chic?
It seems rather Ibsenesque than Pinterish.

Nevertheless, as suits the weather still
In mid-September, I put it on again,
Its armholes needing choosing from its holes.
O spider, standing by the bedroom door-jamb,
You look more diffident than menacing.
Is this your milieu or have you come by chance
From shivering mornings, evenings of westing sun,
Nights of the moon's now powerful chandelier?

From nowhere arrives a vague, operatic thought:
Death may appear in a previous century's garb –
A wig, a sword. Just as my dressing-gown
Could serve productions in 'modern dress', and so
The drama back to the Greek antique – a play
(That may exist) about Arachne, who
Her amorous tapestry unfairly bettered
By the cross goddess, prophetically hanged herself –
And including some specialist staging of the Bad
Quarto, the spectre entering 'in his night gowne'

(Threadbare perhaps from sleepless hours of hell).
What curious worlds myself, if not quite yet
The dressing-gown, have lived through, compelling trends
Of art – white-visaged, sharp-nosed boozers, odd
Headgear, French newspapers, deformed guitars.

In Spengler's terms, it was my destiny,
Rather than merely being by birth inserted
Into a certain time and place and race,
To buy my gown from Jaeger in my heyday
And wear it long as Prospero on his isle.

And as to periods of art, I read
The 'night gowne' quickened Goethe's interest,
The unexpected quarto being discovered
As late as 1823. I stalk
Out on the battlements and overhear a ticking
From still-green trees – the orange-breasted bird
Far closer to being immortal than the play.

Old Themes

Written for Critical Quarterly, *twenty-five years old*

I see in daytime beside the bed my bedside book
and think, with a gush of happiness that astonishes,
of night, the absent middle night of insomnia
that often stretches over dawn, as though full of joy.
When analysed, the promised pleasures are merely that
of reading, near life-long as makes no matter, and that
more recent of old-age, the sense of not being dead.
   The book's Victorian, volume of the *Curiosities*
of Natural History by Francis T. Buckland
(one time assistant surgeon in the Second Life Guards),
my son's gift, doubtless designed to feed my peculiar Muse.
That, a more comprehensible reason for sudden delight.
   Eventually, on my way to bed, occur a few
W.C. Fields routines: to wit, my progress brought

up short as the swinging cord of my dressing-gown drops
through a chair-back's narrowing slats, the massy tassel held;
and then by the garment's cuff engaging (as I switch
out the kitchen light) with the opposed door-handle, in parallel.
    And sure enough, I wake at two, take up the Colonel.
Despite my lust to live, what strike most forcibly
are mortuary passages, also much to Buckland's taste.
'Coffins are generally made of elm, because they last
longer in damp places than any other wood.'
    Of course in the end I have to try to sleep, and fail.
Gone, pleasures of the night; arrived, anticipation
of rotten day – though still a hope or two: that my wife
will waken; wildly premature breakfast send me off;
and, sentinels against utter dottiness, hot milk
plus pills with didactic emollient nomenclature,
emblemed like characters in Jacobean masques.
And somewhat apropos, in Buckland's pages I read
that at the Abbey reinterment of the remains
of surgeon Hunter, between Wilkie and Ben Jonson,
it seems 'the skull of the latter was freely handed about':
grisly, slapstick reward the unfamous nonetheless envy.
    My friend Don Stanford, authority on Robert Bridges,
has pointed out the metre of *The Testament of Beauty*
is primarily iambic. I think myself to try
those 'loose alexandrines', by his pronouncement reassured –
for I'm still governed by the so-called 'model of the language',
scarcely able to verse save through that urgent beat.
But Bridges himself found it hard to scan the *Testament*,
asking friends to tell him of lapses into pentameter
(reminds me of the occasion donkeys years ago,
interviewing Arthur Waley on the wireless, I sometimes
failed to agree the measure of his translated lines).
    Why don't I take the model from my heart? – which like
Bridges has made irregular every foot in the line:
atrial fibrillation through thyrotoxicosis.
Great mystery, prosody; akin to life itself.
I hope not to be cleared up, as peculiar stones
by Buckland's collector father ('this great Geologist')
were proved fossil excrement of extinct monsters.

from *Mianserin Sonnets*

Dreams and Art

Art is to try to impart a narrative
Less boring than dreams. What ought to be removed?
Not all the personally lived and loved,
Nor dotty twists; indeed, the latter give
A deal of art its only excellence.
There are some dreaded dreams that always start
Down a familiar road. Perhaps years apart
Fresh points are reached, with effort and a tense,
Irrational emotion. Who can say,
Until such dreams return, why their feeling-tone
Seems drenched with destiny; the brevity
Yet length of seven decades? Blindly by day
We eat the myriad y's of herring bones;
Sleeping, our stars hang on the garden tree.

Symphonic Dances

Tomato cut in half: wrong-coloured Ace
Of Spades surrounded by exclamation marks.

Having against the odds remembered to
Unplug the lately-charging mower, I

Feel I can now unexpectedly expire
Without undue disaster. In any case,

Low-lying weeds would continue to escape;
Rachmaninov emerge whoever lowered

The stylus in the groove; the pattern, though
Completed, warmingly repetitive.

I wouldn't mind if I were labelled 'the
Composer in D minor' – so I think,

Subsequently supping on a cold
Corpse and some fortune-teller's warning cards.

Death on the Heath

Somewhat melodramatic to think of dying
Here on the heath, with rooks and seagulls crying.

Nevertheless, there comes a Hardyesque
View of my figure, suddenly struck down,

Lone and supine in London's emptiness;
And all I feel I've still to say unsaid.

My father taught me not to be afraid
Of kippers; how with the backbone one was able

To bring out other bones; slide in and lift
The blade to set the opposite bones free.

Of course, had he survived till I was more
Than eight years old he would have taught me more.

The kippers augured well: I still avoid
Choking to death over the breakfast table.

Dimensions

The spider, cunningly cocooned all winter
In a corner of the bathroom, never woke.

One can't help feeling envious in a way.
The eyrie goes on getting blacker: who

Will dare to pull it down? I read that infants
On a glass floor will never hesitate

To crawl across a chasm. Shall we thus
Go into our eternal bathroom coign?

From the same text it seems the cosmos is
Symmetrical in some fine, abstract sense.

I've never doubted my affinity
In the natural world with even the grotesque;

Prepared to die in no more dimensions than
Three bathroom planes, chasms irrelevant.

Is God a Mathematician?

A plethora of abstract algebras.
Where do unusual girls get clothes to match

Their looks – such as these narrow drab-green cords
That elongate the elongated legs?

Does mathematics, describing reality,
Possess unreasonable effectiveness?

Whence comes authority for poetry
To claim its relevance to human life?

One really knows, alas, the enormous worlds,
Escaping, exploding, have little to do with us.

Though possibly obeying the rules of reason.
The masses think art a pain to be avoided

Yet algebraists invent their algebras
Simply to play with: as poets poetry.

In the Park

A pretty girl; walks badly. Almost a précis
Of character. A not so pretty girl;

Limps, brilliant eyes. Perhaps more words required.
A tricycle named 'Bullet' takes its time

To allow me entry to the park. On this
I speak to the driver, with lost irony.

Some girls now dress as though preparing for
Ju-jitsu: precaution needless in my case.

Robins confirm their will to sing again;
The autumn crocus burns its jet of gas

Deep in the heather. Humans lay out their parks
And put on vainly shape-disguising garbs

With what intent but art I'd like to know –
If art can triumph over slouch and eyes.

The Powers

The chestnuts are ejected by the tree
So vigorously I'm surprised, and stay,

Like a village smithy, under the spreading boughs.
Obeying some dictate of geometry,

The husks split in a zig-zag, show inside
A cleanness not excluding stains of birth.

And as the fusillade goes on, I see
The progeny's force derives from gravity –

Comparatively weak, most enigmatic
Of all the powers that rule the universe.

How lucky to be able to describe,
Even withstand, the sniping of the gods

From their elysian, cerulean attic
Well represented by the October sky!

Anatomy of a Cat

Yes, it seemed camouflaged, that brinded cat:
One eye as if completely absent, tail

In several pieces – the squatting shape blocked out
In black and tan and white, appropriate for

Witches' familiar. I don't believe
The cat in *Macbeth* a simple tabby as

The commentaries imply. 'Brinded' is burnt –
In patches – charred, inflamed, exposing bone.

That Wittgenstein thought little of the Bard
I see's to be discussed in some review,

Although experience shows it doesn't do
Even to pass points over in the text –

Much as one wants to trust philosophy
From an old deckchair in a Cambridge room.

Down Kaunda Street

Kenya revisited after forty years!
But only in Nina Casimati's *Guide*.

Why didn't I view more the Kenyan part
Of the 'vast fault' that deeply wounds the earth
Between the Siberian lake and great Zimbabwe?

It seems Nairobi has dual carriage-ways –
Maybe the road that led in former days
From the camp to Lady Delamere's canteen;
The road one travelled standing up in trucks,
Across the Senecan night-time of the plain.

I fail to impose on my shapeless memories
The rigour of the city's Yankee grid.
Besides, most names are novel: I may well
Have been shampoo'd by the Asian Sweeney Todd
In what's now Banda or Kaunda Street.
But even then the future could be divined –
The empire's break-up – more through our tender hearts
Than contemplating military defeat.

Despite its being exile, I came to love
The strange land. The vocabulary of
Swahili given here brings back emotions
Perhaps I never truly owned again.
In retrospect, quite startling I was then
So intimately interlocked with humans
And malevolent devices that could hurt.

What friendships torn in two, myself quite blind
To anything (when at last the moment came)
Save the long voyage to the *patria*!
– Where now the commonalty's going up in flames ...
Lit by dark citizens of Rome, their names
Half Latin, who never clapped eyes on Africa.

Kwaheri Kenya, 'cradle of mankind'!

Questions of Entropy

A few grave questions rise still. Shall I ever
Possess a soldering-iron of my own?
Is it next door a true or false acacia?

I soldered (not soldiered) in the War, was never
A proletarian before. Unknown
Most trees to me, townee, as desert Asia.

Thank God a lot of fellows write in prose –
I think in the middle of the night, when verse
Would be a quite too gagging brew to absorb;

And might bring queries I try not to pose,
Such as how every night makes matter worse,
Despite the mensual splendour of the orb.

The Scale

How near the human, the animal!
How much nearer, the senile or insane!

The cat chatters at me as I defend
The birds whose bright eyes recognize

But little approve of me, like girls.
Are we a caricature, we old,

Of the human; or truly human? A few
Years, perhaps, before one descends the scale.

Touching

'Ne me touchez pas, ne me touchez pas!'
– Mélisande, *très* womanly.
Still to come, the truly disastrous
Results of touching. And finally,
Eager obedience
To that feminine command.

Booloo

I

The islands of that ocean are dispersed
As planets, likewise capturing the sun
Among a vacancy of deepest blue.

Some are mere asteroids: such I landed on.
Landed! – a cutter from the plying ship
Dumped me at a rotting landing-stage.

A choice of three guest-houses, as I'd heard.
Since Charley's droshky was already by
The quay, I went to Charley's 'Number Two' –

Though later found that Sula's put on three
Good meals a day. However, soon I moved
Into a rented 'deteriorating cottage' –

Phrase almost euphemistic what with bats
And rats; and above the ground-bass of the rain
Drippings playing various tunes in tins.

'Doing a minor Gauguin,' so they said.
One felt more a convict or a mutineer;
At best dependent on the shipping-line's

Profit and loss account, or even whim,
Or the world's taste for coconuts and such,
To get back to the life one had renounced.

Still, over drink, a man might tell you when
They sailed in with the novelty of axes;
Times before girls had necklaces of beads.

Kava, the local tipple, but narcotic
Rather than alcoholic: numb effect
Of the dentistry I bravely left behind.

The colour of dark chocolate, Kava, quite
Gratuitously nasty, so no wonder
I quickly contemplated other vices.

I used to sit in trousers in the wavelets
(That made once-grubby toe-nails pink as shells)
To cool off, sober up, while congregated

The solemn or grinning children of the isle.
And soon I hired my twelve-year-old, and was
Domesticated as in times gone by.

Uxorious – long hair, with sea-flowers crowned!
And even fewer words to hold my mind
Than bourgeois girls had uttered in the north.

She thought my dollars counters in some game.
Well, this was usually the view of more
Sophisticated follies of my past.

But was it the linguistic barrier,
Or poverty, or skin that made me think
I could as negligently return with her

As with a Gyppo valet or Chinese cook?
To what? Suburban stuffiness, looking out
Over the city's illuminated hills

To where a kind of other life goes on
In talkative cafés, with booze no more
Consolatory for being subtly hued.

– The stoic poet once again; perhaps
An even greater failure, certainly
At monstrous risk in amatory affairs.

Only too late I saw how happy she
Had been after I'd bought her in the isle;
Status assured, the 'cottage' above her station.

II

She soon expired. The civilized microbes were
Impossible to fight. In her native land
The highest rank alone have souls, and so

She may have never travelled more. And, since
The corner where her sepia remains
Were buried now is utterly overgrown,

Often it seems mere fantasy (as though
The bodying out of my neuroses) that
She ever lived, and here. I might have caused

Her name to be cut into churchyard stone
Had I been sure of it. 'Booloo' I called her,
But that was just half their word for drawing up

A dress, to cover modestly the shoulders,
And meant in that form any adhesive stuff.
Poor, dear Booloo, how well you stuck to me,

Except when proving your people's idea of death –
The intervention of an evil spirit.
At that long drawn-out time I couldn't help

Recalling when was washed up on the shore
A whale long-dead, the stench so terrible
Only the lowest-born would venture close

To cut out the numerous and precious teeth.
Yet you could be concerned about Bulotu,
The now distant island Kingdom of the Dead –

An island like that ocean's other isles,
But where no solid food is needed, merely
Shadow-food (already apt for you).

Its air, just as deliciously perfumed
As whaleless island shores, is nonetheless
The air of Death, unfitted for mortal lungs …

And so that smudge of smoke's abstruse emotion,
When S.S. *Dugong* returned at last to exchange
Its trashy novelties for your devotion,

Turned out to be unhappiness – for me
At least: your voyage, marriage, house of stone,
Assured (you told me) your status for Bulotu;

Only remained to find some craft to take you.

The Marcellus Version

With thanks to James Fenton

Pass me the water. Yes, I played Marcellus.
You'd think I'd not at my age want to cut
The wine, but life seems something now to cherish,
Having survived its sotted years, and roles
Even more dim and ill-paid than Marcellus.
'To be or not to be?' Eh? There's the point.
'To die, to sleep, is *that* all?' There it goes.
You get the answer simply by surviving.
There's nothing after death, not even dreams.
But life's worth living. Yes, despite the fact
That wives die far too early or too late;
And rotten luck; and botched ambition.

It must be twenty years ago he came
And asked me what I remembered of the play.
Nick Lang or Ling his name; and then a dog
Called Sims, black-fingered printer from the City,
Took down my words. Odd's blood, the longest sessions
Of canting and Canary ever known!
I'd been a quick study, quick also to forget.
Whether the fellows knew this, who can tell?
Or why they lit on me. There was a haste
To be the first to sell it to the gulls
And play it in the provinces. Quoth I:
'What part for me?' 'Marcellus.' 'Goblin damned!'
'Also the doubling in the pantomime.'
I took the ducats for my memory
And let them toil to Preston with the play.
I stayed in town. Worked, yes, but rested more.

Anon I met old Whatshisname in Southwark –
Who'd played Corambis on that very tour –
Complaining of a cropped and mangled script,
Not knowing (what a hoot!) the text was mine,
Nor thankful for a part so full of juice,

And lodging in great houses with all found.
He claimed the play had been new printed – twice
The length of my dredged-up memories (the liar) –
And with the ancient hight Polonius,
A part he well might never play again
Since he was, as t'were, for ever Corambis.
Seems Ling and Co had got the bard's foul papers
(Lost at the time the villains came to me)
And set the whole boiling. Proliferating fumes
Of the sack-soaked lunatic poet in his study!

But all that was before the interim
In which babes turned to heroines. My son
(Dead Susan's child) once played Marcellus, and
The servant to Coram – Polonius.
And now you've lugged along a new-born whale
(Anyway, darling, broad-backed like a whale) –
A folio of plays, and all (it seems)
By Shakeshaft. How this would have astounded him,
Who loved the book-trade rather less than I.
And your inserted digit marks a place:
'To be or not to be, that is the question.'
Aye. Well. I see. The poet makes his points.
But note, the length is not much more than mine.
In Preston or, indeed, the City they'd
Have hissed the author's original traffic, yawned
At the coiling of his sub-plot.

                    Bloody cold,
He made it feel on the battlements, admitted.
And by-the-by, even in mid-career
He didn't always get the ictus right.
Give me the tome again. Look here, for instance:
'Touching this dreaded sight twice seen of us.'
Somehow you've got to stress the 'twice' and 'us'
To bring the sense home; yet speak trippingly.
What's left i' the jug? No, no, the wine, the wine.

from *Literary Footnotes*

Felicity

Feeling the felicity of being
At once part of and passenger through
The universe, I wonder how
To capture that second of deep seeing.

And can't help grinning at the far
Image that rises in my sane
But excessively literary brain:
Driving in Edith Wharton's car.

Amatory Dreaming in Old Age

I dream you've left me. And what can bring you back?
For I am as I am; you as you were –
I've nothing to offer beauty, not even rape.
My heart, my entire being's sick, for there's
No chance time or the world will change my lot.

I wake, and wonder if phantom vanishing still
Implies my jealousy (at some suave god
Handling the tender flesh I thought I owned)
Or, worse, prefigures death, the final wound
Inflicted by the capricious female will.

Preserving

Making the marmalade this year, I carve
Some peel to form the initial of your name.

Perhaps you'll come across it when I'm gone,
For even in mourning mornings will go on.

So such surprise as ancient love contrives
Will change to the kind of shock that stunned our prime.

Ward 1G

I

October's end: a glow of sun by day,
And carmine dusks; and moths adhering to
Night-blackened windows – leniencies to match

Your scaffold-timed reprieve, that's also mine.
Even a crew of wasps comes out to take
A final sip of *nouveau* apple-juice,

Bask in residual warmth. Against the light,
The gossamer rigging of a ghostly barque –
Even of fairy complement – is glimpsed.

The apple leaves are dry beneath the tree;
A butterfly settles like a medal on
My breast – a bassoon emerging from the *tutti*.

The setting moon is half a lemon slice
Of dubious imitation sweetmeat fruit
Among the yellower, more regular

Rilkean roadway chandeliers. And what
Than lingering roses in the sodium glare
Can seem more ambiguous in their physique?

I must instruct the video to record
A programme, while I visit you in Ward
1G: a similar device enshrines

The time set by providence for our demise;
Although I can die happy, as it were,
Now you've revived the cliché that life would lack

Meaning without you. Constantly forgotten,
The lesson's re-taught – fear not, crunch away:
The apple-grub is mostly made of apple.

II

The foyer of the district hospital,
The corridors, the wards themselves, confirm
The gulf between the *condition humaine*

And contemplative life, as though one yet again
Were being called on, contrary to desire,
To serve the armed nation, a will outside oneself.

Noting the plaster that attaches you
To various tubes, I wonder what's secured
By a finger's band – and see your wedding-ring.

III

Then it's the time when mad dogs on the heath
Loom through the darkness, followed by their masters:
Devotion by the human to the brute.

On my way home a usual cat miauls
To get my nails beneath its stropping jaw,
Flea-bitten probably; yet rewarding service.

And gratitude to enigmatic powers,
Malevolent on the whole, wells up as I
Return to music's marvels, while you lie

Rather too closely still to the realms of Dis.

Another Art

One more inevitable dusk descends,
Shortening already gravely shortened lives.
How can the little kitchens comprehend
The rosace pattern in a carrot slice?

To indicate the darkness of the heart
Brahms simply had to omit the violins.
But then we often think another art
Is easier than our own to wring and rinse.

Small wonder that the white-hot crescent near
The zenith's navy-blue receives a mere
Glance, though its phases well may represent
Some artist's work, if of obscure intent –

The light and colour, however astonishing,
Our human apprehension of the thing.

Lessons of the Summer

1

Cruel barbarians still exist in lands
Of termite hills or roaming herds; and worse,
Among the meant to be reassuringly
Out-of-date architecture of finance
Houses.
        Quartets of 1799
By different hands, heard on the radio,
Are like a long-standing marriage of quite ill-
Mixed partners, each determined not to die.

3.46: the birds begin to sing.
It sometimes seems to me I merely lack
The patience to compose myself for sleep.
Time to switch off insomnia's wasteful lamps.

Suddenly, in an ephemeral pool, small eggs
Moisten to a soup of fairy shrimps.

2

Carrots haired sparsely as old age; light-fleeing
Earwigs from opened deck-chairs to the grass
Plunge suicidally; tree-seeking birds
Reveal their inexperience of glass,
And purple berries already stain their turds;
The night wind seems a supernatural being.

Haymarket: the façade of the Theatre Royal,
The yellow stucco by the evening lit.
Within, long years of tosh and masterworks.
Buses convey the formicine from toil
To suburban nature, where the notion lurks
That species' adaptations are unfit
For a planet prone to regular cataclysms,
Harsher than even earwig-plumbed abysms.

3

The mowing-machine, as if some deity,
Propels or slices the windfalls indifferently.
The tedious duty's lent some interest
By the appropriate thought that providence
Might well ordain this half-hour to pronounce
The failure of my threatened heart at last
And lay me neatly along a stripe of green
Contrived by grasses bent by the said machine.

But I survive to playing a tape at night –
Starts with two snatches: Bechet, and a terse
Though sumptuous specimen of Korngold – far
Pre-films. Then that last work for orchestra:
Out of the blue a tennis-ball alights
And sends a shiver through the universe.

4

The feminine of blackbird, common brown
Like many girls and beauteous nonetheless,
Runs in the garden teasingly up and down.
Her mixture of biffing and timidity
Reminds me of her human counterpart,
Closer to me in metaphor, alas,
Than ever likely now in reality,
Physique so vilely matched to tender heart.

I eat another Jersey with regrets,
Knowing the longevity of starving rats,
Proved in the scientists' mad lair. But then
Already I'm more than three score years and ten,
Entitled, after all, to strip the rondure
And taste the yielding ivory in wonder.

5

Shiny-skinned cherries, paler by far inside;
Greengages, fruit of little men of Mars …
Eating the food of summer – a race with greed
And mould.
              The title of a *valse* by Liszt
To a princess of vanished ardent years:
'Formerly' – notion Chekhov might have expressed
In groves of birch or some Black Sea resort,
The sunshine coining or burning sad characters.

Despite, perhaps because of, being there –
I mean the human (pot-hats and parasols
And brown girls with their underclothes of white) –
The Eastbourne wavelets were transformed to art.

In empty towns shirt-sleeved old fellows stare
At nothing much. Teatime for porcelain dolls.

6

The end of summer (and perhaps of cities)
Presaged by withered grass on tops of walls.
The heart beats slightly faster on its lattice
Of bone at suchlike Tennysonian symbols
This season of the year, ostensibly
The most removed from mutability.

The light's switched on before the evening meat.
I fear the gathering martins will exhaust
Themselves before their journey across the vast
Mileage that separates chill death from heat.
But, after all, the genus was made for flight;
And, following supper, the air outdoors is quite
As warm yet as any bird might ever need
To sing throughout the day and night, and breed.

7

The robin's song takes over from the wren's.
It strikes me that the shadows of the leaves
Are out of focus through some cock-eyed lens;
And I marvel at the span from shed to eaves
Of gossamer, then notice her who weaves,
Enormous, at the centre of her plans.

It seems there never really was a state
Of infinite density – no surprise to me,
Who've always in general found the infinite
Distasteful, to say the least. Not that I see
The start less puzzling if that theory
Must be rejected. And even I will ponder
Why matter ever had to come to be,
Let alone make these things of special wonder.

8

A leaf nods and betrays the starting rain
That marks the end of gardening for today.
I cut off just above the worn-out knees
The legs of some Terylene and cotton pants,
So made them into shorts, the fashionable
Ragged look. My oldster's extremities
Seem even more ridiculous indoors.
Mere weeding makes me out of breath, and so
With double relief I cover up my shins.
And over tea read Kenneth Clark about
The irony, pessimism, free technique
Of what he terms, Germanic, 'the old-age style';
Doubtful I've had or have a style at all.
Perhaps great song may echo when I speak.

9

Drops regularly fall between the slats
Of garden seats. Another rotten summer.
I used to squander them, now I make the most
Of streaming-windowed afternoons, and don't
Care much if next year and the next are wet
Or perishing so long as I'm about
– Although, a further ice-age on the cards,
One doesn't want to linger on too long,
And have to try to shift oneself and all
One's muckment from this worsening clime to where
Tyrants now rule sweating indolence.
A pigeon flies down with water-darkened breast.
I turn to get some bread to throw: a god,
Typically unreliable, even mad.

10

Two summer 'Pieces for Small Orchestra',
In boyhood heard on a ten-inch 78,
Appear in a Beecham disc remastering:
Exaggerated, my old boast I knew
Every last note of Delius's score.

Obliterating and enhancing Time!
The family philistines, forced to listen as
My school-friend spun the shellac repeatedly,
Are dead – he, too, who did in fact outlast
Our closeness by a decent lifetime's span.

A hover-fly seems interested in my watch,
Rests on its face. Yet surely it must despise
These crude divisions of its single day.

Summers conjoin, of the present, of art, the past.

11

The starlings have started chuntering in the leaves,
Saying the summer must be past its best.
A weed's uprooting from the terrace stone
Brings out some ant eggs which the ants take down,
After uncertain panic, to their nest;
So still the season owns unfinished lives.

How close, these sudden mushrooms to the lawn –
The stalks as stumpy as the legs of pixies.
Holiday postcards come from lands of vine.
It's sobering, apropos at least the reds,
To know I'll never drink the '86s –
Which thank God won't amount to much if their
Weather is half as vile as ours this year.
The annuals die like old folks in their beds.

12

What's happened to the tender lettuces
Of old? I pick up and let fall the tough
Bottle-green bushes passing themselves off
As cos; the tightly coiled varieties,
Tasteless inside appropriate cellophane.
Has one endured pre-summer dependency
On chewing through the uniformity
Of hothouse hue and limpness all in vain?

Art almost at my birth began to fail
To represent reality; just as
Free verse reduced the cunning of the muse.
But never did I think to see a vile
Viridian masquerade, with still less chance
Of a return to tasteful skill, and sense.

13

Martins are busy still between the trees:
It might be their arrival, not their going,
Except a leaf or two's suspiciously
Sallow. The season also tabs the Boeing
Above them as landing in a period's close.
And magpies in the malus – blue, black, red
And white flag of some *outré* party whose
Seizure of power must surely be short-lived.

Clichés accumulate of the decline
Of crucial September, not to say one's own.
Who isn't envious of the mere thirteen
Songs of Duparc, body of work all lean?
Ah, to destroy one's stuff and still survive;
To keep quite silent in gaga later life!

14

I take some summer trousers to be cleaned
Although it's mid-September. Nor do I
Count in the least on wearing them next year;
Quite the reverse. It's just a kind of passion
For order that outweighs my parsimony –
The superego vanquishes the anal.

Fatal to write about September in
September time. As Wallace Stevens said:
Nothing on earth is deader than yesterday's
Realistic poetry. Can't I elevate
My trousered verse? Claude Monet on the beach
At Trouville gave the stripes in girlish frocks
Eternal life less through the shapes defined
Than by the force and sparsity of paint.

15

I meet the self of previous summers in
The scrutiny of phenomena that mark
Time's voyaging: one fallen apple leaf,
More variegated than the fruit that hangs,
Brings flooding back a far, anterior life –
Stronger, intenser (however we old men
May marvel at the everyday), like Bach
Unvariegated by chromatic Liszt.

Sad, the mysterious ordering of things
That makes for increasing complications, then
A sudden return to nakedness – the theme
Simplice, even *religioso*; a twist
Not contemplated by those dawnings when
The myriad parts came in; now like a dream.

16

A spider, nimble but pudding-stomached as
A wrestler from Japan, ascends a thread
I've severed inadvertently, while seeing
To burning stalks ...
                    And so the hours pass:
Even in retrospect, not much to heed,
Though sunlight's at the equivocal stage of being
Filtered by filters about to be destroyed,
Yet powerless to warm bones most in need.

6.45: an empty evening sky,
Great calm, some robin-song. And then I spy
A demi-moon beginning just to glow;
Of unexpected size, indifferent, low.
If time stayed for emotion, what great tears
Might occupy the hours, and moons and years!

Teatimes Past and Present

I allow some creamy milk into my tea:
Reminds me of my mother suddenly
(Dead and gone for approaching forty years),
Who usually poured the top into a jug
To add a luxury to the cup that cheers.
At once incredible and clear, the lag
Of reality behind the lapse of time;
I write with strange feeling the long-unuttered name.

I didn't think to say at any stage
'I'll not forget you.' My undemonstrative
Nature, besides, could never show the love
That unaccountably blossoms in old age.
Or, rather, accountably; having no need to prove
Itself, except on the inhuman page.

The Hairbrush

I came across my father's hairbrush, mine
Almost done in, and cleaned the silver back,
Discovering an elaborate intertwine
Of 'LCF' beneath the decades' black.

I feel the bristles, as he might have felt,
Against the scalp; the more acutely for
Some years of brushing with a mangy pelt.
Thus swallowed up are sixty years and more.

– Although my hair is not so thick of late,
Whereas my father's close-curled when he died,
Likely to scorn the severest brush's grate;

Unless I'm suppressing the guilt of parricide,
And months of unjust malignant suffering had
In fact made sparser, as in old age, his head.

The Elderly Husband

Once more a lenient December: is
It really the case that I am spared to try
To burn what fell when she was at death's door?
I hear the usual robin as I rake;
I have to quit the smouldering when the dusk
Announces strangely that it's time for tea;
A quince of summer crunches underfoot;
Below the rot a gold or even green
Sprouting prognosticates the still-far spring.
I bear a cup to her, then guiltily
Over my own hear Gerald Finzi's work
For cello that illegally I've changed
From air to tape. What gods can possibly
Exist to whom thanks must be breathed for this?

Bird of Passage

Strange journey home, after a West End day
Of work in others' company, with drinks,
Coffees and lunch; my diuretic pills
Withheld of necessity – so waterworks
Subject to hope as frail as prayers for rain.

Capturing a bus, following a wind-blown wait,
I'm forced at length to disembark on shores
Unknown, and seek a pub, and use its apt
Convenience; then sally forth as though
I'd patronized its profitable wares.

Music was playing, the tables mostly joined
Mixed pairs. The marvellous relief was all
Too quickly cancelled out by feeling like
A sparrow flying through a feasting hall.

Oneself

How curious that at seventy-two one still
Expects to be fulfilled and understood –
Perhaps on the coming of a near event –
Having been disappointed all one's life.

Of course, in sober meditation one's
Aware how little time remains for things
To change their nature, that in fact one is
A creature for ever simply of expectation.

Being alive and moderately happy –
Merely a habit. 'Moderately': how
Dare one thus qualify the lack of pain;
Hearing in Haydn's witty silences

One's dearest not unhealthily cough, as one
With optimism versifies again?

Nature Programme

Viewing a nature programme on TV,
It strikes me: one existence, and to be
Swallowed alive, entire! For even now,
At seventy, my death I can't allow!

Yet every hour I'm conscious there's no law
Ruling continuance – that a random jaw
May dislocate itself and slowly take
Myself to the digestion of a snake.

Though how can the living truly realize
What nature's programme is? That light-planned eyes
Should sense eternal dark, and the unbrave
Body sustain an unrelenting vice –
Merely poetic wings and feelers wave
Feebly against descent into the grave …

Dans un Omnibus de Londres

1

Mid-afternoon: some winos plot beneath
The canopy of a ruined cinema –
A 'modernist' survival of the years
We thought of indifferent quality, now seeming,
In popular morality and art,
To have sustained what we shall never know
Again. A dirt-steeped figure, bottle raised,
Crosses the pavement, but my bus moves on
Before I can enjoy his tiff with traffic
Or thoroughly identify with him –
For here one's might-have-been is given shape.
The cinema itself is like a temple
Of civilized antiquity after prolonged
Years of barbarians. Too much is wrong.

2

A loose dress may imply a slender frame;
Neck be no shorter than a long coiffure.
Strange that front teeth just overlap front teeth –
Though one's as far as can be from calling up
A grinning skull. In their erotic life
The blackbirds are far more discreet than sparrows.
The fashionable footwear tends to slip,
Below the almost non-existent calves.
Too young for adult manners, yet too old
To quite avoid the taint of coming ills.
Passengers are exchanged like a losing game
Of beggar-my-neighbour as we journey out
From urban street to suddenly widespread green;
In which I'll be deposited, discreet.

3

Gesticulating against our history,
Who are you, horsemen of the square? Before
The pious plinths can be deciphered, we
Swerve off to cross by arches the stream that here
Was fordable, perhaps by elephants.
And so began the city. Bogus, all
These very obviously subsequent
Riders; and not because of seized-up scrolls,
Or swords that couldn't slice a pound of butter,
But in most cases the equestrian role
Itself. For though commissioned and raised by utter
Arseholers, art shows pot-bellies bodying out
The armour; the incongruity of control
Of chargers by tiny heads, conceited snouts.

4

The upper deck: a seat behind a bitch
That looks out through the window with such angst
Or anticipation that I see its tongue
Droops over its lower fangs like a Dali watch.
Its forepaws on the window-rail are odd
Contraptions of seeming rubber and mineral,
Unhandy for holding on, as is the tail.
Nevertheless, a much worse article
Might well have been bred and house-trained down the ages
Under the species expounded by the peaked,
Uncomely passengers I see around.
But is the beast still capable of rages
In which it laps with relish what has leaked
From whores and tyrants dashed to the ground by God?

News of the World

The seaweed-eating sheep of Ronaldsay;
Don Giovanni set for wind octet;
New Zealand hedgehogs strangely lacking fleas;
And Poincaré's Conjecture solved at last:
How can this world end through the human will?
(Although we know the destiny of stars
Is to explode or cool or fatally
Devour their very farthest satellites.)

Yet courier after courier arrives:
'They sank our ships within twelve miles of shore';
'The latest fashions are to hole the ear
In divers places, and to cram the toes
In shoes as narrow as the serpent's tongue';
And 'God's mad vicars war like infidels'.

from *The Cancer Hospital*

Your Absence

During your absence, when I swept the floor –
A long grey hair among the household dust.
An empty room, two petals by the door –
Relics of what mankind appears to trust
When flesh is failing, though nature equally
With art needs human health to keep its place
In human consciousness. Catastrophe
Shows more of its veiled but ever haunting face.

Darwinian miracle, that now has gone
Somewhat amiss, I see is not mine but yours
Alone to go on holding, or to lose;
Although when I receive at length the news
That you're to live I find another cause
For living, and realize I needed one.

Postscript

My hands are burnt through cooking, by roses scarred.
It's taken your illness and the carelessness
Of age to join me with the working-class,
Though in the war I used to skin my fingers
Crawling in aircraft beached in arching hangars.
The war! – unknown to possibly a third
Of present humans, including those whose wrong
Organs convey them to the Fulham Road
Early as middle-age. The way is long –
Shortish for some – and up and down for most.
Even insomniacs, if tired enough,
Eventually throw off their wearying load.
Available for dreams: a mighty cast
Of all the dead and living of my life.

Minor Keys

I

The mountain spewed; made twenty thousand dead
But this was merely to anticipate –
For some, less horrid than more usual fate.

But all the draft poems, sketches for finished oils!
– Destroyed by fireballs, under rivers of mud
For ever sunk. Good job the artists died

Ignorant of their loss, Carlylean
Catastrophe only the dotty great could bear;
Or so I think, far from hell's aperture.

II

Sometimes I wish that I had strung together
The meditations of my later life
To make a poor man's *Prelude* or, more like,

Recluse; although the lack of genius counts
Little in nature's cruelty. Indeed,
I feel that once or twice along the road

I somehow got on paper comprehensions
Of rarest emotion, suddenly-seeing eyes,
Aeolian response to melodies.

III

A puddle holds a sky cracked by the season's
Denuding branches: elsewhere in the night,
A moon new-born, though able to stand upright.

Sunlight's a fading yellow in the west.
Just left behind, in Friday's Vanity Fair
Of lighted streets and shops and motor-cars,

The pure yet human beauty of the young –
Still mousiness-unthreatened golden hair,
Responding like some crop to parents' care.

IV

The poet's character: is it any stranger
Than the rest of man's? The predilection for
Puzzles and conjuring; and touching fur …

I wonder if it's really morbid, eyeing
Comb-marks and brush-shine. Certainly, very few
Note down such items as that Martinu

Was influenced in 1945
By old-hat Brahms; that Freud preferred to call
His patients 'students'. Am I well or ill?

V

To think of art in the context of disaster!
Already I may have blabbed my secret hope
That, say, in the South Seas Lomaiviti Group

A faithful fan exists who has assembled
My works, and so despite atomic war
They will miraculously pass entire

To the survivors – surely more numerous
Than those on this overcrowded earth who now
Deign to imbibe my sub-Wordsworthian brew.

VI

Leaves having fallen, lit windows reappear
Down vistas from the evening house and lawn.
Voyeurs can see my antics from dusk till dawn.

The pianola proves that even in
(Perhaps especially) the notorious
Prelude Rachmaninov rolled the chords: one must

Be just as moved that Erroll Garner does
The same in the disc of 'Misty'. Random emotion
In a random season – see Uncle Tom's 'Gerontion'.

VII

And yet ... On the radio I hear a fellow
Articulate the start of Mozart in
G minor, all too often rushed: again

The exploding fire and engulfing mud
Take their subsidiary place, although
Defining where the race of men must go.

Happiness, the final aim of art,
Is always, as we know, too good to last.
How else came minor keys to mean the most?

Summer Laughter

Summer laughter from the gardens
Teases ancient ears.
For the season-ruled potato
The end of scraping nears.

Abundant swell the shapes of summer –
Ridged marrow, pea canoe.
Earth's mighty waters weep like captives
From cucumbers cut through.

Suddenly-ripened berberis berries
By birds' insides are drained,
Blotting the virgin garden benches
With droppings purple-stained.

A thermal whirls a few initial
Leaves in their later coat.
The maestro has to croak in wisdom
Phrases the girl must float.

Nasty Weather Ahead

Pollen in peat bogs;
The age of the herring,
Grape-fat years.

Gigantic advance of Alpine glaciers,
Crushing of villages round Chamonix;
Drying out of the once cyclonic Sahara.

The fourteenth and fifteenth centuries –
Dire crises. Then warm winters
Of economic revival, Brazilian gold.

Great thaws, ending of great wars,
After the Sun King's demise.
Who suspected governance by

The circumpolar vortex,
Or minuscule variations
In our axis of rotation?

The future: nothing left on earth
To feel enough terror
At the abrupt return of ice.

The failure of the Gods –
Not to like men.
Thus the failure of man.

Note: The poem is indebted to Emmanuel Le Roy Ladurie's review of H.H. Lamb's
Climate History and the Modern World (*Times Literary Supplement*, 21 January 1983).

Metaphors

The 'golden age' of hell,
The hell of the Baroque –
Billions of bodies mouth
To mouth, amid a stench
Mephitic. From my book
I look up, shocked that some
Experienced in our time
That hell, not just in art
Or under the pulpit's lash,
But on east Europe's plains.

It seems that earthquakes force
Earth to spin faster, through
Compacting it the more –
As skaters faster spin
By tucking in their arms.
The metaphors of man
For the true nature of
The universe must amaze
Even its god. Who dares
To say: incinerate
A chair, and no chair-soul
Can possibly remain?

Advice to the Elderly

Like November's great blue fly,
If the day is mild go forth,
Though the sole blossom (of
The ivy) a mere green pseudo-flower.

Keep house contentedly
Should the April wind stay north:
What will come your way of love
Now past the exercise of power.

The Envious Poet

Even as I swallow a crimson tablet of erythromycin
To kill the cohorts of evil invading my chest, I feel
Regret that I must leave to painters and composers
Areas of art I've always longed myself to fill,
Although about to quit my own art unfulfilled.
I see that to depict the trailing foreground of leaves
You let the dark-green dry before applying light,
And that the quality of melody is even
More vital for success in quick parts than in slow.
But what to do about it with these wheezing words
Would take another lifetime to sort out, to say
Nothing of needing a more capacious pair of lungs
That easily would range from deep bassoon to white.

Triangles

I dream you've left me; wake, and find you gone.
The dream was of a rival, falling out
Of love, an anguish terrible to bear.
Waking is almost a relief – to know
We're old, so old such triangles must be
Quite ludicrously far into the past;
And if there's a rival he bears a common name
And merely sits beside you in the ward.

The Letter

I see from the envelope
Your fingers formed my name –
The personal row of letters
Written by those new carrots
Ending in gnawed-at horn.

Nothing more intimate
May be expected after
The envelope is slit –
From the epistle's subscription
Nor its assignation.

Venus, Mars and Cupid

To rub the pane and startle Venus, apart
On navy-blue, and in the electric blur
Divine her actual phase! This month the star
Pursues and even catches gory Mars.

I dozed off earlier in the day, my dreams
Making their fresh arrangements of the past:
My son, escaping nude as Cupid from
His bath, before the war that severed us.

How soon, my standing in the holy fire,
Far from the consequences of desire!

My Life

Soon, no one will remember my eccentricity –
A fair example, fitting 'Oh Dearie me today'
(The catchphrase of a childhood landlady)
To the tune of 'Lady Be Good'.
And who else will echo my grandfather's phrase
Of assent when offered a second helping:
'Just for amusement'.

The hairy torso has collapsed beneath
The somewhat less than right-angles
Of the octodic legs.
Spider, art tha sleeping there below,
Or dead? Perhaps it may come to be said:
He was a man who used to care about
Intruders from another world.

I see my life's immense alternative –
Wife dead in childbirth (as she nearly was)
And I in the ensuing war with thus
Less motive to try to save myself from the worst.
As it is, I'm older than my grandfather,
And most days making fresh discoveries –
That Rimsky wrote Rachmaninovian songs;
How martins gather under a sky of greys;
And down a garden wall a snail
Moves rather quicker than a minute-hand.

Later Sonnets from the Portuguese

Beholding, besides love, the end of love …

I

The poet watches fat beneath the grill
Blister from white to brown, a quantum shift
Reminding her of Nagasaki's skin.

One of her bread loaves sticks: a bit is left
Behind – a jigsaw piece she must detach
And turn to fit in the appropriate hole.

Weeding a bed, she discoveres broken glass
From a war she hardly witnessed. Why not be
The fifth or sixth to write 'vastidity'?

She wants the world to be more like herself;
Yet, copying any corporal, files her cans
In ranks of size upon a kitchen shelf.

And takes a book up when chores cease to press:
Shaxberd's *Mesur for Mesur* in modern dress.

II

Fatherless children, poems – more or less.
Her natural progeny in crueller ways
Were orphans. Tears well up; she dabs the cambric.
The slumbering cat reminds her of the days
When suddenly a noisy child slept thus
(Odd moment, deathly sleep) and she was free
To write of the Permian catastrophe
Or, say, pre-Cambrian times – assorted tripe
Miraculously blending into verse.
But who knows when inspiration's over-ripe,
If time must make the poet's language worse
As it inevitably brings the placid?
O great deoxyribonucleic acid!
– Even the molecule of life's iambic.

III

Rulers and sexual partners in disguise –
Foreshadowing the Vienna of later days,
Freud added to its 'timeless monuments'.
She looks up from the ingenious final wonders
Of reconciliatory transference;
And not entirely incongruously ponders
How long since she felt the fuzz and amazing warmth
Of unclosed skull against her open mouth.

As in the case of comradeship and war,
Of motherhood the memory retains
Only felicity. Outside, a pair
(Content upon a bough) of collared doves –
The number of happiness in diverse loves
It well may be she'll never know again.

IV

The elder bushes emanate their being
From fleurets mainly greenly beaded still
(Full foam to come), like waves far off from shore.
Surely she must have versified before
The catspee scent, just as she's always seeing
A blackbird's angry downturn to its bill.

'He hath but as offended in a dream'
– The words remind us that the work is set
In Freud's own city. How extraordinary that
Not only human dreams but human lives
Are acted out amid both canvas trees
And things that are quite simply what they seem.

Empires and schools of melody today!
– Only the pastoral resists decay.

V

Undoubtedly offputting, those extrusions,
Resembling the body's interiority;
In some moods she wants easier illusions –
Perhaps platonic nights … or even years.

Sayings of lovers: You are like a fox,
Smaller than I imagined. And then harking
Back to affairs before they even met –
Opposite poles of verse and jealousy.

A sudden shower: the slanted roof-tops smoking
Beyond the blue and exhaled grey of his.
The masculine – almost too crude to stand,
And yet she stood it, as do all her sex.

Jack Palance in the movie, *Chato's Land*,
Avowed: 'We stay till the 'pache breed is hung'.

VI

Unfortunate, the anguished botheration
Of parting should coincide with inspiration,
When often in art life's commonplaces tell.

The starling's body now is almost gone,
Ravaged by flies and ants, and saving her
Distasteful offices of burial.

The universe is young, or so aver
Fashionable astronomers – less than
A dozen gigayears. So what's to come
May yet outgrow these really quite insane
Contingencies of flesh and blood and brain;
And, singing voices made for ever dumb,
The cosmos settle exclusively to nice
Or wildly unstable packets of fire and ice.

VII

It's early summer: in the garden tree
Green embryo apples have uncannily
Appeared, in somewhat science-fiction mode –
Invaders from outer space that must assume
Organic forms to prosper on the Earth.

Her daughter was determined to be born;
Precaution, steel, mandragora, evil stars
Proving quite powerless to prevent the birth.
How infinitely reassuring, the force
Of tiny seed – of infancy, and youth!

She all at once seems to see the truth of things
(Slicing tomatoes with a saw-edged knife).
O fly, escape to other flies! She flings
The window open, as though upon her life.

VIII

A spider dreams away the day and night
Below the clothesline, just beyond the pane.
Various beasts squeeze underneath the screen
That marks the boundary of her back domain
(A vanishing ambiguous tail is seen) –
Area illumined by the kitchen light.

The spectral moonbeams fill the silent house;
Vanished the whimpering brood and snoring spouse
It's almost as though her years had never gone,
And she feels ready once more to take on
The making of a unit in the nation;
Though the small hours show her habitation
Shared only with such as silverfish. The ridge
Of background snow is freezer piled on fridge.

IX

The Duke (she thinks), no less than Angelo
And Isabella, apt analysand
Of Freud in the later city. What deep woe
Carlylean wisdom may conceal! The banned
Desires – one upright furrow in the brow.
No purgative, not rhubarb nor yet senna,
Can rid her of memories that make her now
Merely 'a looker-on here in Vienna' –
The actors in the drama of her days
Gone forth to take the lead in other plays.

Could she live on if passing eyes ignored
The outward form presented them to see
(Beauty she owned so long it almost bored)?
And yet they do that thing; and so does she.

X

Her father and his politics came from times
Surely of more illusions than her own,
Rather as her children's folly seems
Folly to her and little else. Between
Those who released the atom and those who now
Appear forgetful of it, she exists,
Appropriately middle-aged. But how
Unfit she'd be to inhabit either era!

Chicks seem enormous once they've left their nests.
After his heroic years the father
Shrinks. In this stretch of life, mere passing showers
Confine her to her solitary room.
Almost as good to visualize the flowers
As live through the week or two until they bloom.

XI

To her surprise she saw his poetry
Develop – seemingly having thought herself,
Not least in parting, the one essential Muse.
So winter went and summer again came by:
No more the garden a background for the wolf;
Lavender was vibrated by the bees;

Three mushrooms sprouted on her unmown lawn.
She wishes she could always have been free
To say: 'Nothing repels me.' But, of course,
Even in their relation's rosy dawn
The seasons revolved, and (imperceptibly
At first) time changed things, as it does, for worse.

And just for the bombus, nature, after all,
Goes to some trouble to set out her stall.

XII

She struck 'amreeta' out as too *outré* –
As though his critical regard were still
Over her shoulder. Can there come a day
When what has been has no great part to play?

And yet it seems not long ago her will
Controlled the future by being dominant
Over the present. Already quite a fossil,
She now sees youth short-sighted as the ant.

You have to live through a morbid lust for words,
And try to write the truth of being down,
And take the cracked potato with the sound –
For as she cogitates, some begging birds
Light on the kitchen window-sill, their brown
Eyes on the potato-peeler in her hand.

XIII

In fact she never missed home-talk and blessing
And the common kiss. New vistas of walls and floors
At once supplanted what she might be missing –
As though she had grown up with dark-green doors,
High ceilings, of a Victorian maisonette;
One adored male, and not a varied shoal
Of sexes, ages, love. And so the set
Of sequent homes, improving, on the whole.
Thus she is left with empty rooms as well
As empty hours. It's only where a knife
Pares parsnips or potatoes she can quell
Her domicile's unintelligible fears.
You switch the light on and a moth appears,
To look in through the window on your life.

XIV

Man is a primate foetus that's become
Through chance of ages sexually mature.
After her bath she ponders the human frame:
Science is not quite sure what nails are for.
Is it her future for no one to care
About her body and its destiny?
Even herself seems somewhat cavalier
As to its tie-up with the essential she;
Though should some peninsula of pain occur
She'd only be too concerned to cut it free.
Quite wolfish, what the scissors make to trim;
May grow the more so as the years advance;
Hands, too, become less assiduous to proclaim
From the wild kingdoms their profound difference.

XV

Her father thought that politics comprised
The quick of living in our modern day;
And so when she grew up she was amazed
To find someone she loved for whom the word,
The phrase, the paragraph, were really play,
And could be as nonsensical as a bird.

Anxiety about far-off régimes,
And whether history is saying alas,
All at once lifted. And arrived the times
When private language seemed an esperanto;
And heroine and hero fell to assess
Themselves in canto after ample canto.
It was as though a voice was speaking: whose
Rule, Fairie Queene's or Blatant Beast's? You choose.

XVI

O frail original and faded bliss,
Faded in retrospect so soon, if not
As quickly diagnosed fundamentally frail!
And while that dwindled, his reputation grew
Not least because that famous work of his
Delineated the emotions hot
From two bound close, from labiate head to tail;
And she herself engendering what was new.

Unlike the Chinese, frogs are really all
The same (or so she reads). Batrachian,
The facts of love – though there speaks middle-age,
Blasé because no longer can befall
Lips breathing on the face like a scented fan,
Or pressing their crimson imprint on the page.

XVII

The wild flower chooses where it best may thrive:
Not always where it's difficult to pick,
For its abundance seems meant to heal the sick.
And man is helped agreeably to survive
By nursing spiky parsley, lengthy chive.
Anticipated like a nervous tic,
The bar of the tune where the drummer drops his stick.
Too amply proving the recording live.

Nature and art: the metaphors in each
At last quite overwhelmed her, whereas he
Was able in these disciplines to teach
The young, and in their compost-flattery
Grew fat and sleek and languid as a leech.
Who's the true sonneteer then, he or she?

XVIII

And as for her, fame turned (to match her themes)
Domesticated; house-bound as a cat.
When her affections were at large, it seems
Her conquest of the youthful literate
Was effortless, complete. No more, no more!
Now she writes only of the fatal flaw
That clatters round regularly, as it were,
Among the improvisatory, to gnaw
The memory with remorse. He moved away
To match his audience with lovers, eloped
To cities she'd never visit, where the day
Was rich with the compost of the night. She hoped
Merely to go on showing existence as
A beetle world deep hidden in the grass.

XIX

Windings of dark acacia boughs, among
Their stippled green – yes, but what metaphors
Can nature lend when love's gone badly wrong,
And living's channelled in its narrowest course:
Mere breathing, eating, sleep (not much of that)?
And what a daunting amplitude of hours
She finds she suddenly possesses, sat
Surrounded by unemblematic flowers
(Although on an acacia bough a dove,
Rather too aptly deserted, squats like her).
Yet she surprisingly wouldn't in a way
Want to re-live her life, neither before
Nor after she was vitalized by love –
Almost repelled by her vanished stamina.

XX

Her outdoors mug of tea steams into sunlight
Angled and partially obstructed, like
(She fancies) a street-lamp filtered through a fanlight.
And does the rhyme-word make the matter true,
Life justified by noting for noting's sake –
As, the inimitable damson hue?
Nearly in secret, the habit of poetry
Went on; was then uncovered, so to say,
By time, and now stands steaming in a cup.
It did not turn in her, 'the thing called love',
To hatred, though that emotion doubtless drove
Him from the house where children had grown up –
Who played among the trees that shaft the sun
In a strange summer of being the only one.

XXI

She used to read from a collected Grimm
To offspring who perhaps were mesmerized
Less by the stories than her voice, and dim
Light and the weariness from play. Good thing:
For often she found that she was uttering
What would have hurt them had they realized
Its import – like Joringel, whose Jorinda
Was changed to a nightingale for ever more,
The culprit an old witch with yellow skin.
Ah, days when she could think herself a part
Of song and sadness, yet with nothing to hinder
Her closing the cruel book and bedroom door,
Leaving a kiss above each tiny chin,
To join the faithful Joringel of her heart.

XXII

Call it ironic that as she lost her beauty
(Prompting him to gaze – elsewhere – the more),
The children's love was damped, then turned to duty;
The relation scarcely better than before.
She thought: my role is changing to the witch,
Who changed the girl into a nightingale.
How long before she becomes a cat or bitch;
And existence cruel, like a fairy tale,
And as unlikely? With spider, moth and mouse,
She sees the full moon shining all the night
Into the now far too commodious house,
And so the opposing panes in turn ignite.
Perhaps it would not have needed the traumatic
To demonstrate her place was in the attic.

XXIII

It seems a last-century medico maintained
That women's reproductive cycle and
The organs of reproduction themselves inclined

The sex to lunacy. One remedy
(No doubt of quite short-term efficiency):
A vulva packed with ice (if that could be).

But apathy, listlessness and inanition –
The classic symptom-cluster of depression –
Who's to pontificate on their causation?

Such act of mourning is a vain revenge,
Since the revengee's then long out of range,
Gone to a sane if over-heated change –

A pale young face in tangled yellow hair,
Clothes that just sketch her as already bare.

XXIV

Its incandescence lights the window-frame,
Then falls indoors upon the rocking-horse
They kept on sentimentally in the room
For long a nursery. She wandered in
(She tells herself) to see the spectral moon
From this now empty quarter of the house.

The forty-four elaborate protocols
Of love were easily within her power
Even in days of steeplechasing toys.
In fact, she felt her vision brooding over
Europe, its millions familiar as the dolls
That populated the present ghostly place.

Now she looks up enviously on this eye
That tirelessly views all stuff beneath the sky.

XXV

Illyria, the girl was living in –
Sadness of mourning brothers; ludicrous sadness
Of thwarted ambition tending near to madness;
Sadness of clowning, of being daft and thin;
And yet perhaps was always a suspicion
That things would work out happily some day,
At least for the chief *dramatis personae*,
With whom she was numbered in her secret vision.

Yes, life showed itself a comedy, despite
The Learish father, and suspenseful Acts
Before the astounded, unlikely, happy greetings.
But, looking back, whose would be now the right
Collected volume to enshrine the facts,
The play proving not to end in lovers' meetings?

XXVI

She was amazed when one day, one specific
Day, showed his love for her had gone – in fact,
Changed to disliking almost as terrific
As once had been the feeling it replaced.
She never considered then that she had lacked
At times, across the years, the constancy
Of ardour that alone could justify
(It might be said) the extent she was amazed.

Emotion makes one's head ache, she thought after.
The solitary tears did not come back:
Instead, a constant unanticipation
Of joy fell on her; no exaggeration
To say like one on Death Row or the rack;
Affecting even the return of laughter.

XXVII

Sleeping prefers the proxy of the wish
And not the evil wish itself, like art.
It jibes, that she was once a dozy bard.
Then came the cobweb-breaking, wakening kiss.

It was as though another father had
Appeared, so how was she to know at first
A war was pending; so to speak, the fists
Of rival sons – two from the primal horde?

Love loves to swear to last until – beyond! –
The grave, and, if not, then falls short of love.
Though who need swear for ever to be fond
Of issue? As for them, they merely strive
In curious ways to go on loving those
They hugged with freedom in primeval days.

XXVIII

In dewy mornings she takes up her pen.
The damsons come and go, and after all
Their crimson stain proves not indelible.
She'll leave behind her in her *oeuvre* – and *vie*! –
Trace of the 'primal insatiability'
Of her desires; or so she hopes. But then,
What novelty? For common to all human,
The loss of being once a part of woman;
And that she has indeed bequeathed already.
Against her face the evenings now are thready
With webs – between the outhouse and the line,
Outhouse and damson-tree incarnadine.
The corner-loving spider in this season
Sits in the centre of its spangled reason.

XXIX

Putting dried peas to steep, one pea pops up:
A poet, a freak from a contented mass –
Content to be drowned and tenderized and at last
Devoured. But this (part brown, a half-size pup)
Makes as to escape its siblings' destiny.
Of course, now she could wish that when he kissed
Initially he had, as it might be, missed.
Her sex at first is inclined to acquiesce
When faced with pouring, hot emotion, just
As the pea-consensus. And when apparently –
Years later, that seemed a dreaming quickly passed –
His passion changed to hatred, once again
She could do little, like the chimpanzee
Who quite lacked grammar, though had learnt to sign.

XXX

She ducks the webs like a boxer, and feels sad
When sensing an alien thread among her hair
At dusk. If only all the animal –
And human – kingdom had such respect for right!

But plainly the Primal Cause built in the bad.
And she herself is conscious that in her
Are both the timid scuttling and the evil
Of binding and sucking dry the free in flight.

Entering the night-time kitchen she has seen
The cooker's pilot-light's mysterious glow,
And then perceived that even the washing-up
Possessed its worlds of supernatural sheen.
Past bitterness, the draining of a cup –
Simplicity of all that we can know.

XXXI

Occasionally he sadly wept as well.
Tears of the crocodile, she thought, and may
Even have said. If so, no wonder they
Are living he in heaven, she in hell.
Or, rather, she assumes his happiness,
Exaggerates her misery. Of course,
it was no lack of sympathy in the head
(Which speaks and takes rough words with smooth) that led
To such exchanges – simply the theorem
That shapes of women that appeal to men
Are strict and pre-determined. She and he
(So must have been her assumption) were exempt
From law, and she imagining also the
Perennial lure of beauty beneath contempt.

XXXII

The lime tree's fruit, with helicopter blade
To ensure its scattering, swivels down,
The ancient pawnbroker's sign in miniature.
It startles her, sitting in sunlight – like
The tiny warnings once unseasonably
Falling from the blue into a happiness
That subsequent October-like devastation
Turned into grief.
                         It seems a legend now,
When even autumn's fragility was part
Of a robust commingling of life and art,
With waiting winter merely signalling
The sleeping seed under a springing heel –
Humans with every month in which to sing,
And art no more desirous than the real.

XXXIII

She thought him the superior at first –
Astounding time of the genius of youth,
Which is to believe as well as state the truth,
However best turns later into worst.

– Partly because he was her rescuer.
From what? All kinds of ill, most past recall,
Supplanted by a set it looks will all
Endure till her demise, and gather more.

She wakes and finds the bedroom curtains lit,
And thinks about the content of her dreams.
The house, still, will remain so till she stirs.

Among the rest, her daemon also quit,
And only ever comes visiting, it seems,
In these half-fathomed Brontëan nights of hers.

XXXIV

First, the unloading of her woes on him,
Then the discovery of the griefs he bore –
Which his lent strength enabled her to share.
Nothing much gathered by the brothers Grimm
Excelled the happy outcome of this start.
And as for their two fames – well, either one
Seemed fed by the other. But then, later, stones
Instead of kids rumbled beneath her heart.

As much because of her now slatternly ways
As tenderness to life, the spider stays
Inviolate indoors. How could she change,
Somewhere in the unfolding of the tale,
To a persona it was plain must fail,
Condemned for ever to the kitchen-range?

XXXV

Yet in the autumn life seems specially
Abundant – dancing flies in sunlight, grubs
Dangling on strings, and cobwebs netting shrubs.
The human must respond, and does – though she
Counts it a season towards eternity,
Despite the absence in her world of terror
More than an extra wrinkle in the mirror,
Or twinge she may ascribe to malignancy.

The final wars to come! Moon shining down
On an unlighted, empty earth – a super
Blackout of the kind her childhood knew!
But this may only be a plot on paper,
And nothing worse for her than withering brown,
Even backed sometimes by cerulean blue.

XXXVI

She criticized his verse before his nose.
That is, she saw first she'd been overawed
By talent: profile joined it later on.
Does admiration of the flesh depend
Upon the mind within it, in the end?
The question's like: can bad men write good prose?
To find the trochees and iambics flawed
Prepared her for discovering love had gone.

Epochs of art even by middle-age
Are quite discernible, let alone those of love.
It only needs the clumsy, old-fashioned glove
To be removed, bare fingers turn the page
To a clean place, and suddenly everyone
Is writing like Wagner or Alfred Tennyson.

XXXVII

She sees the spider scurry from the rain
That makes webs tremble. Which purveys the truth –
First or third person, middle-age or youth?
The ancient armies of remorse or pain
Invade her resisting memory once again –
The darling sibling's childhood death somehow
She might have avoided; or the recent now,
When the loving word stayed frozen in the brain.

The events of nature like those of history
Appal their participants; no comfort that
The ruined house is left bediamonded
(Except to impersonal poets who have shed
Their egotism – even what life is at –
In the mad servitude to artistry.)

XXXVIII

The verses that she wrote to him seem now
Quite metaphysical: it strikes her how
Already at such time she was preparing
For the elusive element in caring
That most endures. But who will see through those
Items marmoreal; generalized Rialtos;
Specified vegetation, mainly flowers;
Heraldry, insect life, and even giaours?

The naked moon in all its shapes astounds.
No wonder he worshipped her several names; great wounds
The goddess suffering at neglected shrines.
These later days she easily confines
Her inspiration to the physical –
The countenance's craters lit by old Sol.

XXXIX

She can remember what she wore at times
Happy and unhappy, trivial or tragic –
Matters more apt for prose, perhaps, than rhymes:
The feminine earthbound, underplaying magic.
What he forgot was rather more than ties
And shirts. But who's to judge the quality
Of celebration? As Proust said, nothing dies
That has survived. And each day she is free
To root back in her wardrobe, or go out
To buy a set of memories from a shop
(Though her experience is that a curious doubt
Attends new apparel). Connections never stop.
The assured symphonic period ends; begins
The works for cello, viola, violins.

XL

The quarto compositor's misprint or misreading –
'Crulentious' – rather insinuates what she feels
About her life: vague animosity.
How often in Eliza's reign the bleeding
Of humankind in verse! The comic heals
As best it can the wounds of Acts Five and Three.
But in her own day only the actual
Participants in tyrannies and wars
Appear to be entitled so to write –
Women confined to the girlish or shrewish role,
As scullions must stick to kitchen chores.
The mere perusers of tragedies may indite
Only such detail as a dead leaf blown
Indoors seems a map of some far, desert zone.

XLI

The heroines of Shakespeare: products merely
Of masculine imagination – thus
It seems to her amidst her ruined life,
Despite the dramas' images being severely
Focused on gardens, dogs, the daily round.
She used to think: suppose I woke and found
He had returned? But utterly ludicrous
To contemplate herself a Julio
Romano sixteen years had lined to no
Effect, save to make a more alluring wife.

The daughter who hid her love! Her hatred, rather.
All men are Lears. And yet, and yet – a tear
Started when mortal illness felled her father:
Hard woman's tender heart; strong man's great fear.

XLII

No doubt she could have similarly wept
For the already absent, traitorous spouse.
But now she merely tries to keep mind swept
Of demons, like the dust inside the house.

A spider, hanging bat-like, waits in furs
Through showers and shine to parcel up the flies,
Ending the little lives that might be hers.
Despite its range of beaded complexities,
The web's not there for any human joy.
Dusk coming on, the spider tight-ropes to
Any trapped small fry. She recalls the boy,
As she still often does, the sibling who
Dies in her infancy and his, and haunted
Those of her own, with terror of the enchanted.

XLIII

Life echoes life: husband and father, son
And brother. Through her unshared bedroom ceiling
Water seeps slowly from a faulty run
Of tank and pipe. For like subconscious feeling,
There's brought into a house the pressure of
Entire lacustrine systems. All the past!
Such utter rot, the primacy of love –
Unless self-love, alone the kind that lasts.

And so a man invades her solitude,
To screw the super-ego tight. There spill
Out now mere intimations of the nude
Body of earthly forces: the success
Of insects, say –the external cuticle;
1780: water equals gas.

XLIV

A sphere of gold, a mile in diameter:
If such existed, nature's laws would still
Accommodate it – so she read somewhere.
It follows maniacs abound, among
Whom she would class clandestine adulterers.
Sometimes she wonders if he might be ill,
Before remembering she need no longer care –
The family's end, an end of right and wrong.

She thinks: I could have loved into old age –
A confidence unlikely to be tested.
Long, long ago she wrote an immortal page
And numbered herself among the apple-breasted.
Save in mad kings, how comic-futile rage
Against the rung where the Creator rested!

The Story

Most of the inconveniences of my
Demise will not, however, be borne by me –
Consoling, now that almost anything
Unusual brings with it anxiety.

Often I feel perhaps I don't mind death –
Still free from pain and lameness, despite old age;
And yet I blench to think some moment in
The story I shan't be there to turn the page.

AFTERWORD

Roy Fuller's first book was simply called *Poems*, like Auden's; he was relieved that it had appeared in 1939, making him (just) a 'Thirties Poet'. But he didn't really belong to any decade or group or school, which was liberating for his talent if confusing for his reputation. In making Auden his mentor, he wisely chose a poet who taught more good habits than bad ones and whose work altered during his career; Fuller's changed too. Some of his phases mirror Auden's: thus the wartime poems are succeeded, after something of a lull, by the big reflective pieces in *Brutus's Orchard*, then by the wide-ranging syllabic meditations of *New Poems*, before a late phase of wryly observant notebook-poems. Yet there are huge differences: Auden couldn't have written, as Fuller so distinctively did, about wartime service experience; nor did he live to enjoy a period of immensely productive old age.

Attractive as some of Fuller's earliest poems are, it was the war which shaped his poetic voice, even before he was called up in April 1941: it made him see ordinary things differently. 'The last trains go earlier, stations are like aquaria,' he wrote in 'First Winter of War', which exactly catches the paradoxes of a world both familiar and topsy-turvy: 'It is dark at twelve: I walk down the up escalator ...' It's a world which already wears the colours of combat and has had its military haircut:

> Cigar-coloured bracken, the gloom between the trees,
> The straight wet by-pass through the shaven clover
> Smell of the war as if already these
> Were salients or cover.

That is the opening stanza of 'Autumn 1939', the first poem in *The Middle of a War*; but the war's middle – the book was aptly, and luckily, published in 1942 – wasn't quite the same as the middle of Fuller's war. At that point, he was only just setting off, destination unknown, aboard a troopship from Liverpool; so the collection's main theme is the strange transformation of a young solicitor into a radar mechanic with the Fleet Air Arm, and the apparently long view of the title poem ('My photograph already looks historic') is coloured with his characteristic irony. The unknown destination turned out to be Kenya: this is where the second phase of Fuller's war poetry began, as he turned his attention to the entirely unfamiliar scenes recorded in such justly famous poems as 'The Green Hills of Africa' and 'The Giraffes', from *A Lost Season* (1944). It's worth insisting that these are as much war poems as Owen's or Sassoon's; it was, of course, a different kind of war from theirs, but in each case literate young men found themselves faced with geographical and social challenges entirely beyond their previous experience. For Fuller, close proximity to his fellow human beings at once qualified his idealistic socialism and strengthened his regard for 'ordinary' individuals, while poems such as 'The White Conscript and the Black Conscript' and 'Teba' address the problems of inter-racial understanding with eloquence and candour. But there was to be a third phase in Fuller's war: 'after a journey devised by The Admiralty in association with Kafka' (as he put it in a letter to his friend Julian Symons), he was back in England where, following another bemused spell in naval training establishments, he ended up with a desk job in Lower Regent Street. He marked his return with 'Winter in England', a sonnet sequence which establishes him as a compassionate yet critical observer of the society around him. If his poetic output then seemed temporarily to flag, this was partly because, camouflaged by stacks of naval bumf, he was busily writing a novel, *Savage Gold*, for his young son.

This was the point at which he might have struck out for a full-time literary career; but, after the war, he returned to his old job as a building society solicitor (eventually becoming a director of the Woolwich) and set about establishing a home with his wife and son in Blackheath, where he continued to live until his death in 1991. When I once asked him how he managed to combine his prolific writing life with so different and demanding a full-time job, he gently explained that he could do the one *because* of the other. I took this to imply something like the bookish schoolboy's pained endurance of maths and physics, sustained only by the promise of English after break, but I don't think that was quite right: Fuller enjoyed his work as a solicitor, and the habit of toying with and relishing odd or litigious forms of words adds a special, slightly quirky flavour to his writing. In 1949, the year of *Epitaphs and Occasions*, his first post-war collection, he also published

Questions and Answers in Building Society Law and Practice: he was, as he put it in 'Obituary of R. Fuller', one of several hostage-to-fortune pieces he wrote at about this time, 'Part managerial, part poetic', and there's a perfectly straightforward sense in which he couldn't have been one without the other.

Peace brought its own terrors, as he noted at the very end of the war: 'Now all the permanent and real / Furies are settling in upstairs.' There may have been less to worry about, but there was more time to worry about it; and the early 1950s added ill-health to his other anxieties. Fuller turned to fiction, producing in rapid succession a trio of Graham Greeneish detective novels: *The Second Curtain* (1953) is a masterpiece of its kind and 'Rhetoric of a Journey', the opening poem in *Counterparts* (1954), is clearly related to it. This branches out meditatively from its occasion in a manner which recalls the 'conversation poems' of Coleridge: it's a new and fruitful style for Fuller, of which the outstanding example is 'The Ides of March' from his next collection, *Brutus's Orchard* (1957). Adapting the familiar scene from *Julius Caesar*, the poem is a blank verse dramatic monologue (apart from the last three words), thought aloud by a Brutus who is very like his author and whose concerns, moreover, are as relevant to post-war Britain as they are to ancient Rome. The fireballs and thunder of the opening line eventually subside to a mood of becalmed inactivity; yet, ironically, it is precisely by not acting, by remaining thoughtfully within his orchard until the conspirators arrive, that Brutus commits himself to action and chooses 'what history foretells':

> The dawn comes moonlike now between the trees
> And silhouettes some rather muffled figures.
> It is embarrassing to find oneself
> Involved in this clumsy masquerade. There still
> Is time to send a servant with a message:
> 'Brutus is not at home': time to postpone
> Relief and fear. Yet, plucking nervously
> The pregnant twigs, I stay. Good morning, comrades.

'The Ides of March' is, among other things, a triumph of sustained tone, in which the civilised, understated speaking voice perfectly balances reason and emotion. Had Fuller been ten years younger and represented in an anthology such as *New Lines*, it might have been more clearly recognised, alongside Larkin's 'Church Going' and Gunn's 'On the Move', as one of the defining poems of the 1950s.

If there's a lengthier lull after *Brutus's Orchard*, only partially broken by his first *Collected Poems* (1962) and a relatively slight collection, *Buff* (1965), it needs to be remembered that these were the years in which Fuller established himself as a mainstream novelist – with *Image of a Society* (1956), *The Ruined Boys* (1959), *The Father's Comedy* (1961), *The Perfect Fool* (1963) and *My Child, My Sister* (1965) – as well as being much in demand as a reviewer and as a broadcaster on the Third Programme. Once again, his poetic self-reinvention, when it came, was both decisive and successful. He adopted a high-risk strategy of unrhymed syllabics for his boldly titled *New Poems* of 1968: they were 'new' not just in the sense of 'recent' but because he felt they were different in kind from his previous work. They enabled him to move much further in the direction signalled by *Brutus's Orchard*, often including an astonishing range of material within a single poem. The most audacious of these *New Poems* is 'Orders', which begins disarmingly with a 'visiting quartet' of suburban wildlife – father and daughter blackbird, pigeon, squirrel – on the lawn beyond his study window: a scene we'll come to know as a typical starting-point in Fuller's later work. Yet already something more adventurous is going on, in his casual reference to the daughter bird as 'Cordelia' and in his use of the word 'nature'; between them, they direct us to the discussion of 'The Two Natures' in *Shakespeare's Doctrine of Nature*, John F. Danby's then quite recent book on *King Lear*, as well as to to a key phrase in 'The Visitors', 'the double nature of nature'. Once alerted to the intellectual world beyond the immaculately described scene, we may be less surprised to find Fuller, in the poem's next paragraph, reading (and 'Not really understanding') J.B. Bury and thence moving to the 'nature/nurture' debate of *The Tempest* before jolting back to the present and the 'quite senseless war' in Vietnam. Goethe and Kafka then make appearances as the poem veers, as is often the way with Fuller, towards its cautiously redemptive conclusion:

> And what if ourselves became divine, and fell
> On the pitiful but attractive human,
> Taking the temporary guise of a swan
> Or a serpent: could we return to our more
> Abstract designs untouched by the temporal;

Would we not afterwards try to get back those
Beautiful offspring, so mortal, so fated?

The suggestion that the temporal world is beautiful *because* mortal and fated is a characteristically hard-won reaffirmation of faith in humanity. 'Orders' may sound like a difficult, rambling poem; the miracle is that its intellectual honesty and conversational ease make it a simple pleasure to read.

Shortly after the publication of *New Poems*, Fuller was elected Professor of Poetry at Oxford. There he began to cultivate, somewhat to the puzzlement of his audiences, a prototype of the ironic old buffer mask behind which he often hid in his later years: the two volumes of his Oxford lectures seem a little awkward as a result, but there is at least as much wisdom about literary life to be found in his fine though underrated (perhaps because unhappily titled) short novel, *The Carnal Island* (1970). His next collection, *Tiny Tears* (1973), inaugurated a prolific late period: the spell of almost twenty years which was to include a large *New and Collected Poems*, half a dozen new collections and numerous pamphlets, as well as four volumes of memoirs. The knack of these poems often lies in the recognition, at once troubling and consolatory, that ordinary life is endlessly surprising. 'The Unremarkable Year', for instance, begins by recalling things that haven't happened lately, though soon finds reassurance in the less than momentous things that have:

But there is much to be said for a summer
Without alarms. The plum crop is modest,
The monarch has remained unchanged,
Small differences only in one's teeth and hair and verse-forms.

By the end of the poem, this self-deprecating irony has modulated into something more complex, for 'the year of painting the shed ... Is also that of harmonies / That have made one's life and art for evermore off-key'. That clash of 'harmonies' and 'off-key' resolves into a necessarily imperfect cadence, recalling the compromised lyricism of Fuller's favourite composers.

His remaining book-length collections fall readily into two categories: *The Reign of Sparrows* (1980), *Consolations* (1987) and the posthumous *Last Poems* (1993) are, in the best possible sense, rag-bags without unifying themes or forms; while *From the Joke Shop* (1975), *Subsequent to Summer* (1985) and *Available for Dreams* (1989) are formal sequences, the first consisting of poems in triplets, the second and third of sonnets. For many readers, these three books contain Fuller's most distinctive late work – indeed, they couldn't possibly be by anyone else – but, as John Fuller rightly suggests in his Preface, their cumulative nature makes the task of selection from them exceptionally difficult: 'A sequence builds up its own little body of myths and points of reference,' as the author himself said of *From the Joke Shop*. This doesn't mean that the poems won't work individually, however, and they range from the mildly gruesome lightness of the title-poem (celebrating a lifelong fondness for jokey toys and recalling the doll in 'Tiny Tears') to the wonderfully deft movements between a Blackheath winter garden, autobiography, music and literature in 'The Future'.

The working title of *Available for Dreams* was *Sonnets and 'Sonnets'*, since it contains both true sonnets and other poems of fourteen lines; the book runs to 150 pages. Even more than *From the Joke Shop*, it demands to be read as a kind of quasi-Proustian narrative, its details constantly nudging and resonating against each other; it is also the book in which Fuller most effectively exploits his knack of seeming intimately personal and self-deflating at once. Despite recurrent themes of ageing, illness and despair, it isn't a gloomy book: there remain the consolations, as well as the sheer oddities, of civilised suburban life. There are also, as in the rhymed sonnet which concludes the group called 'Lessons of the Summer', moments of pure wonder at the astonishing nature of things:

> 6.45: an empty evening sky,
> Great calm, some robin-song. And then I spy
> A demi-moon beginning just to glow;
> Of unexpected size, indifferent, low.
> If time stayed for emotion, what great tears
> Might occupy the hours, and moons and years!

I was lucky enough to meet Roy Fuller while I was a postgraduate student, in circumstances which were, precisely, 'Part managerial, part poetic'. The Chairman of the Woolwich, Sandy Meikle, who happened to live in the same Kent village as my parents, had persuaded his Legal

Director to give a reading to the friends of the local amateur dramatic society; he wondered whether I'd join them for dinner, perhaps sensing that the company ought to include someone else who'd read and even written a poem or two. I did my best to monopolise Roy Fuller's conversation during that meal and after the reading: a lapse of manners for which, forty years later, I remain wholly unrepentant. Thereafter, he'd send me neatly inscribed pamphlets and beautifully laconic postcards, with wry comments on my work or on what I'd said in print about his; I don't think anyone could have shown more sustained and tactful kindness to a younger writer than he did. The reader, I'm afraid, will have to take that on trust. But what needn't now be taken on trust, with the appearance of this generous *Selected Poems*, is the quality of his poetry and the pleasure it will give to both old and new readers.

Neil Powell

INDEX OF TITLES AND FIRST LINES

Titles are shown in italic, first lines in roman.